WWW.SNOWPATROL.NET

PUBLISHED 2005
©INTERNATIONAL MUSIC PUBLICATIONS LTD.
GRIFFIN HOUSE,161 HAMMERSMITH ROAD, LONDON W6 8BS ENGLAND.

ARRANGED AND ENGRAVED BY ARTEMIS MUSIC LTD. (WWW.ARTEMISMUSIC.COM)
REPRODUCING THIS MUSIC IN ANY FORM IS ILLEGAL AND FORBIDDEN BY THE COPYRIGHT,
DESIGNS AND PATENTS ACT, 1988.

HOW TO BE DEAD

WORDS AND MUSIC BY GARY LIGHTBODY, JONATHAN QUINN, MARK McCLELLAND AND NATHAN CONNOLLY

3

Verse *Harmony 2° only*

4

want-ed be - fore,__ so sweet-heart tell me what's up, I won't stop, no way.
talk a-bout growth. You've not heard

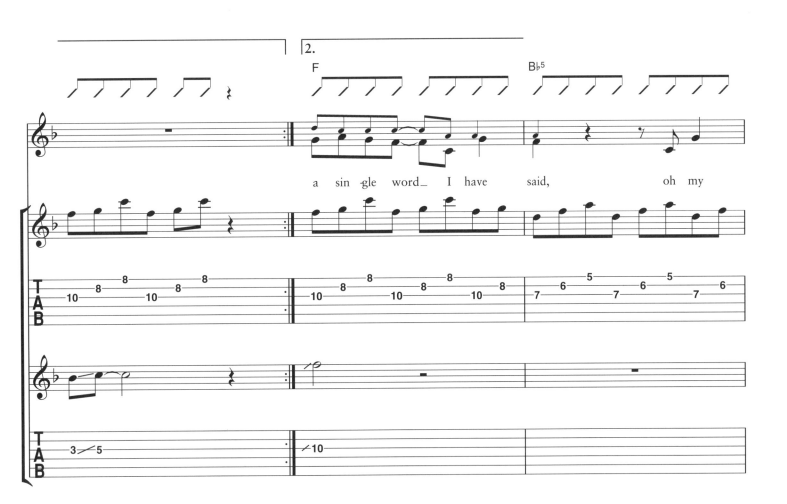

a sin-gle word_ I have said, oh my

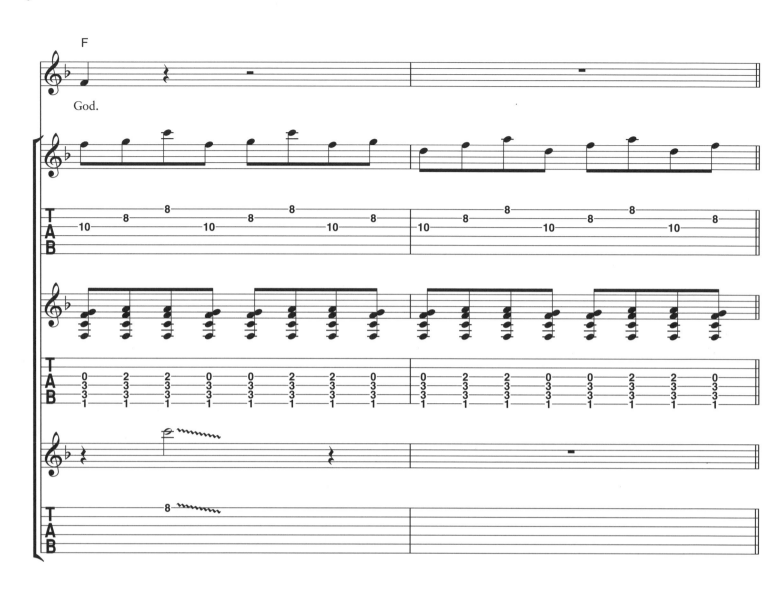

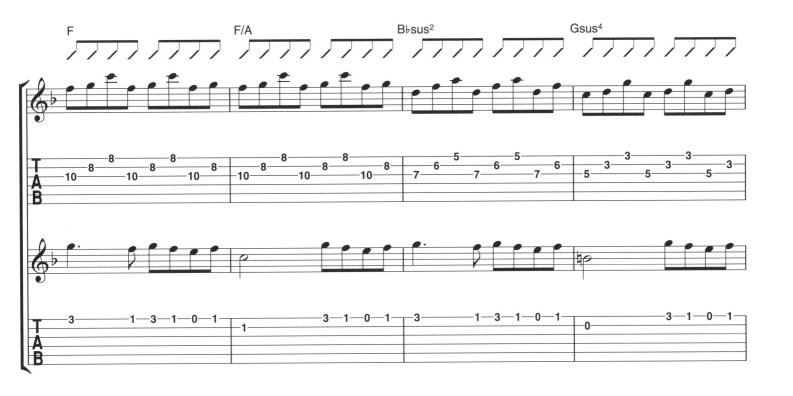

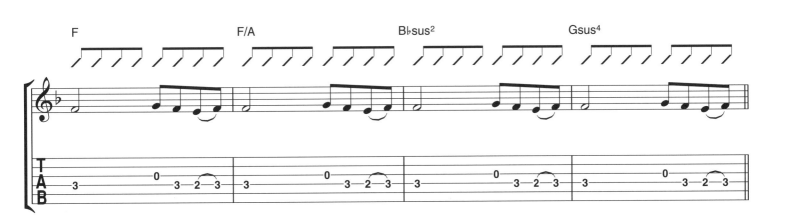

-gain and a - gain,__ but if the ec - sta - cy's in,__ the wit is def -'nite - ly out.__ Doc - tor

Jek - yll is wres - tl - ing Hyde for my

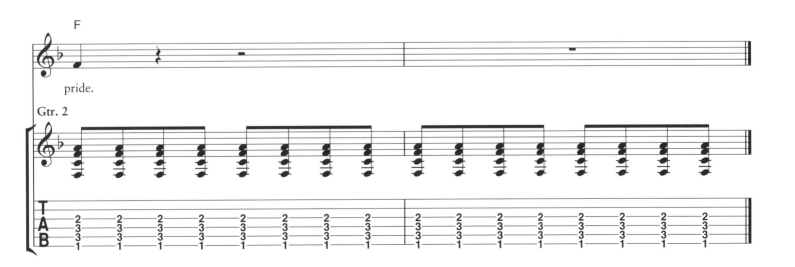

pride.

Gtr. 2

WORDS AND MUSIC BY GARY LIGHTBODY, JONATHAN QUINN, MARK McCLELLAND AND NATHAN CONNOLLY

Free time

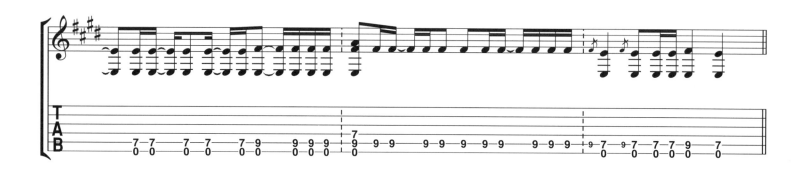

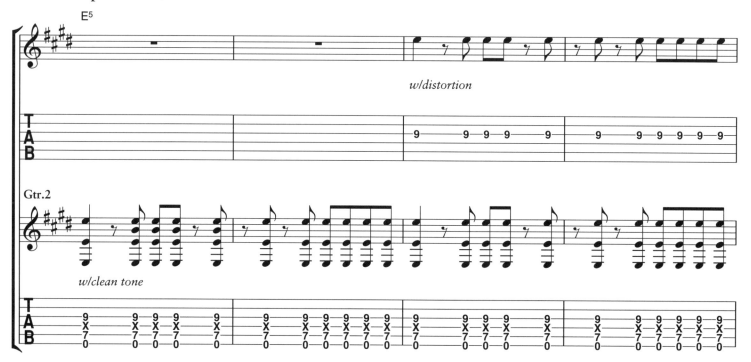

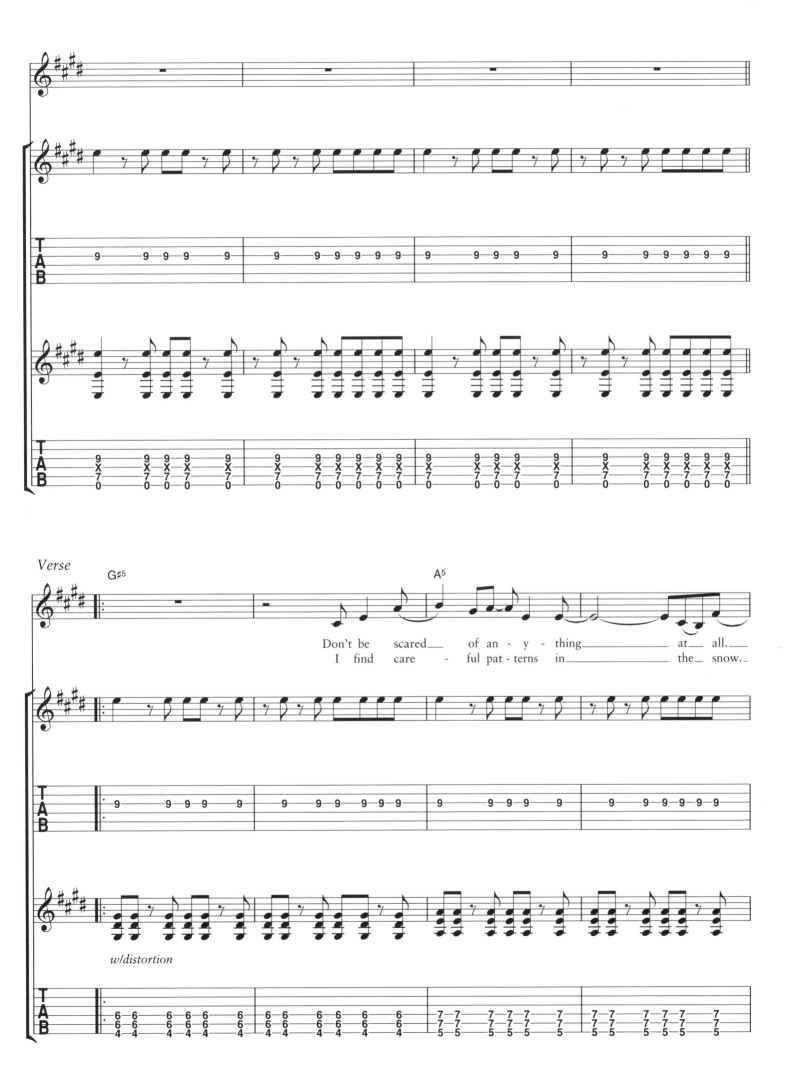

Verse

Don't be scared___ of an - y - thing_____ at__ all.___
I find care - ful pat - terns in_____ the_ snow._

w/distortion

16

To Coda ⊕

A⁵   B⁵   E⁵

All gon-na change,__yes it's all____ go-ing to___ change.

Synth. arr. for Gtr.

D.%. al Coda

All gon-na change, yes it's all___ go-ing to___ change.

Coda

Play 4 times

w/vocal effects ad lib.

GLEAMING AUCTION

WORDS AND MUSIC BY GARY LIGHTBODY, JONATHAN QUINN, MARK McCLELLAND AND NATHAN CONNOLLY

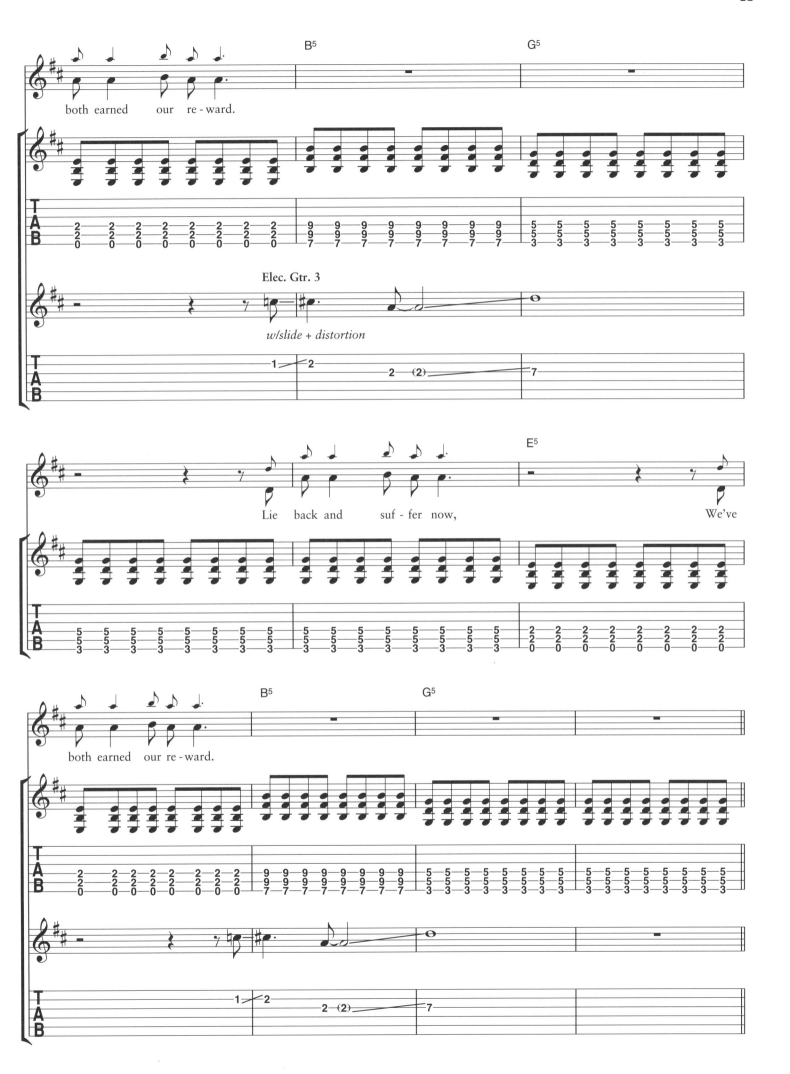

Verse

Bur-ied deep_ in the te - le -gram   I'm sure I   nev - er   got_

w/whammy pedal

— was an - y   clue_ of the where - a -bouts   of   all the   things_ I'd   lost.

Chorus

It's   not   as   sim - ple   as   how
Bro - ken   glass   a - side,   my

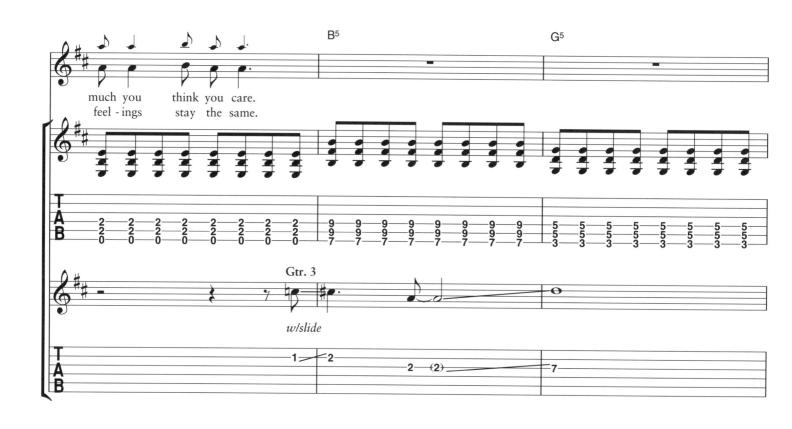

much   you   think   you   care.
feel - ings   stay   the   same.

w/slide

You   would   nev - er   know
Cov - ered   head   to   toe

WHATEVER'S LEFT

WORDS AND MUSIC BY GARY LIGHTBODY, JONATHAN QUINN, MARK McCLELLAND AND NATHAN CONNOLLY

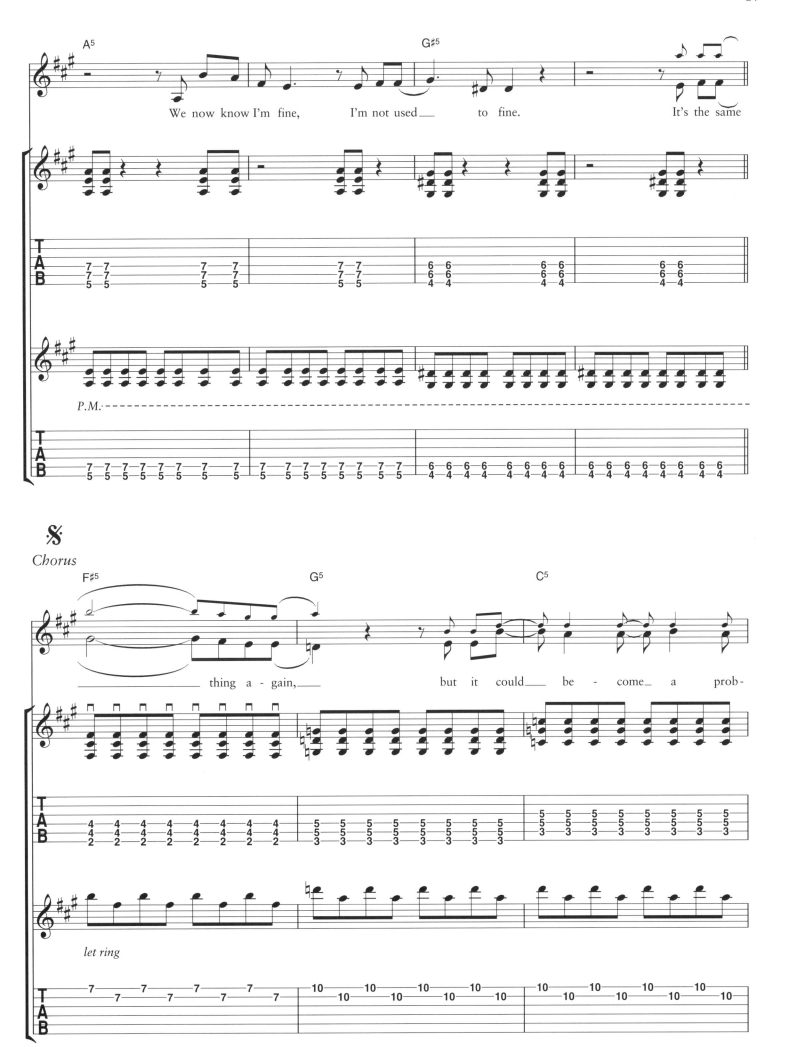

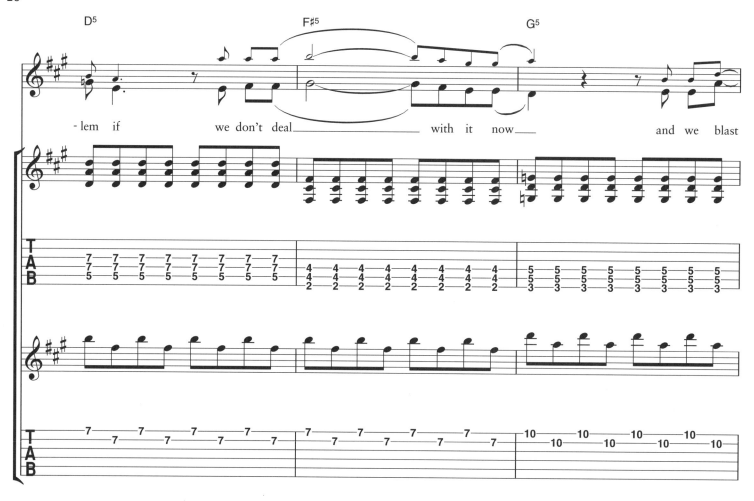

-lem if we don't deal_____ with it now___ and we blast

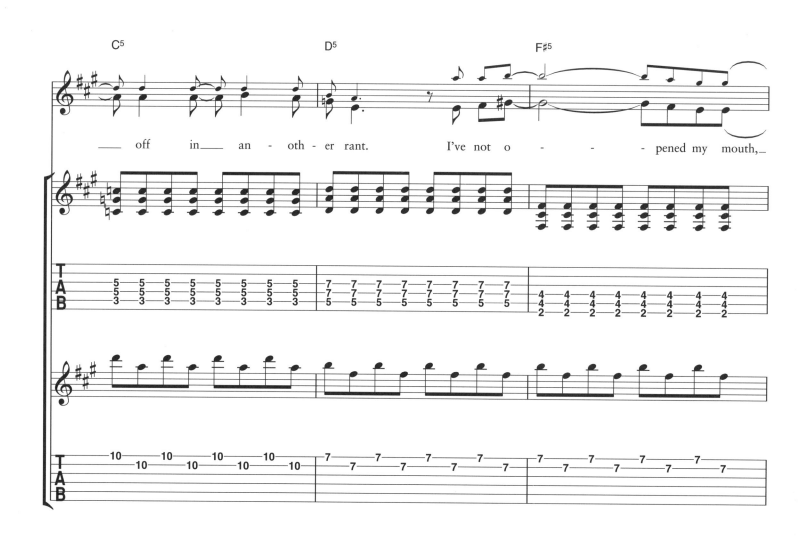

___ off in___ an - oth - er rant. I've not o - - - pened my mouth,___

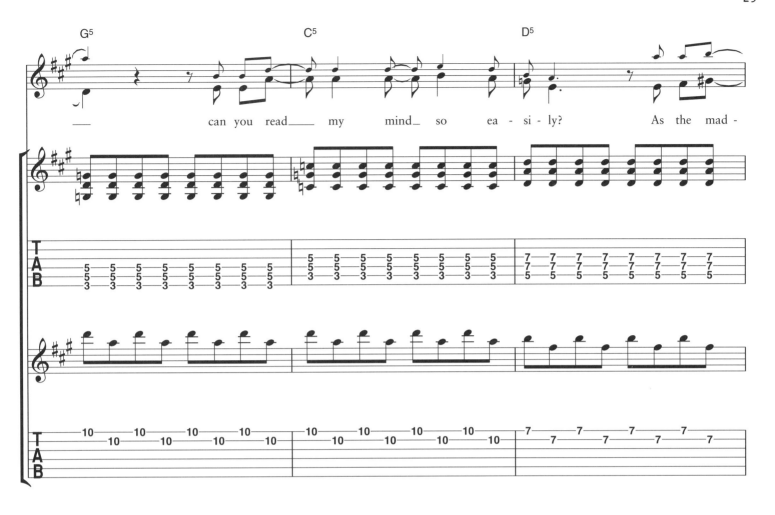

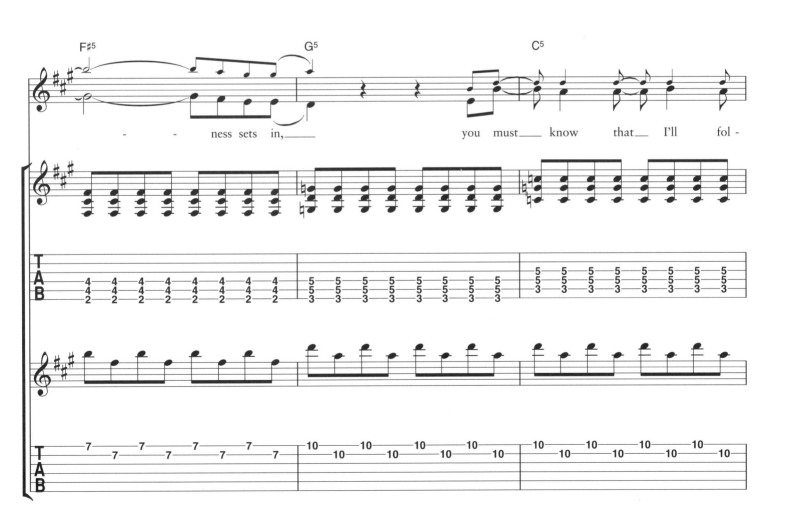

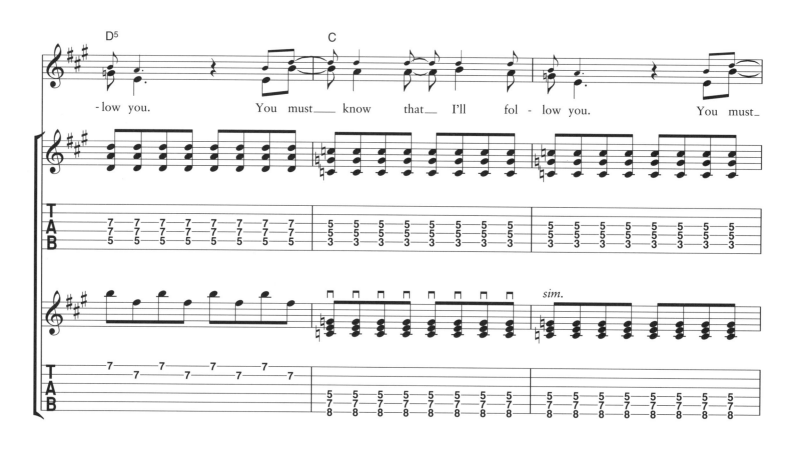

- low you.   You must___ know that___ I'll   fol - low you.   You must___

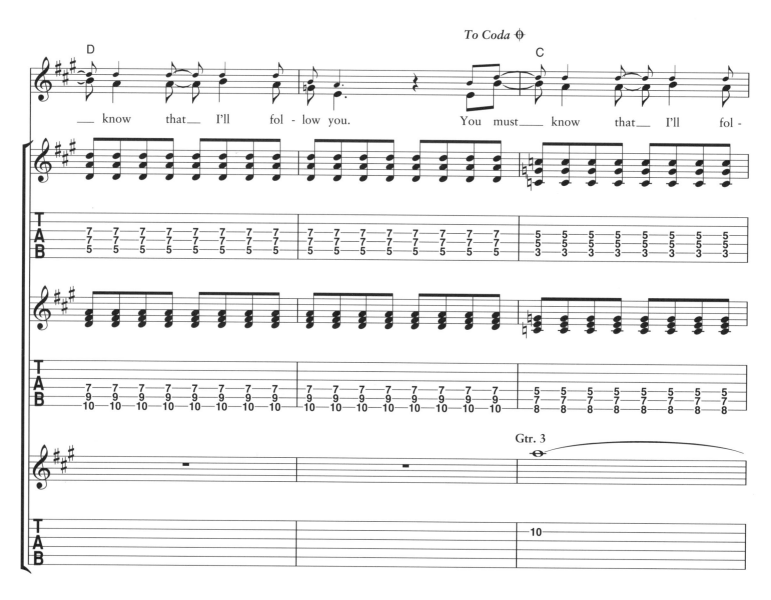

___ know that___ I'll   fol - low you.   You must___ know   that___ I'll   fol -

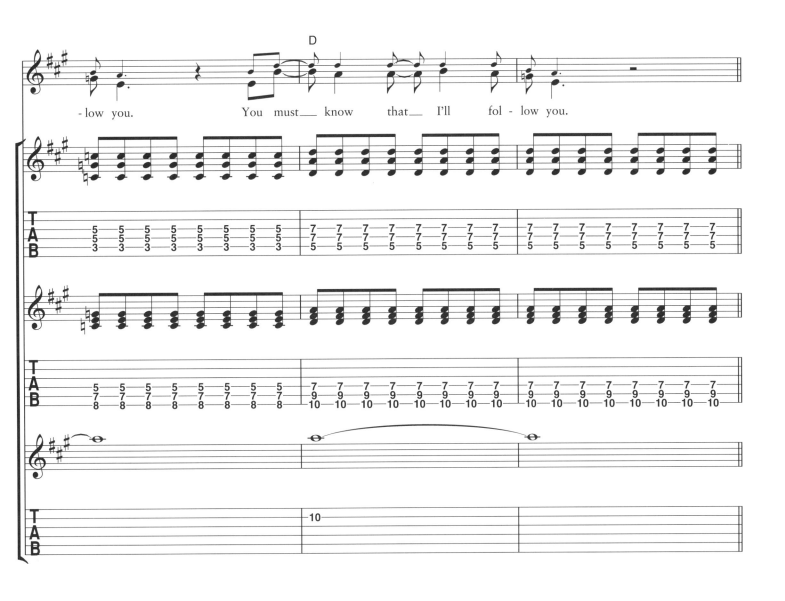

-low you.   You must__ know   that__ I'll   fol - low you.

Verse

A sud - den move - ment   and a bro   -   ken limb.

⊕ *Coda*

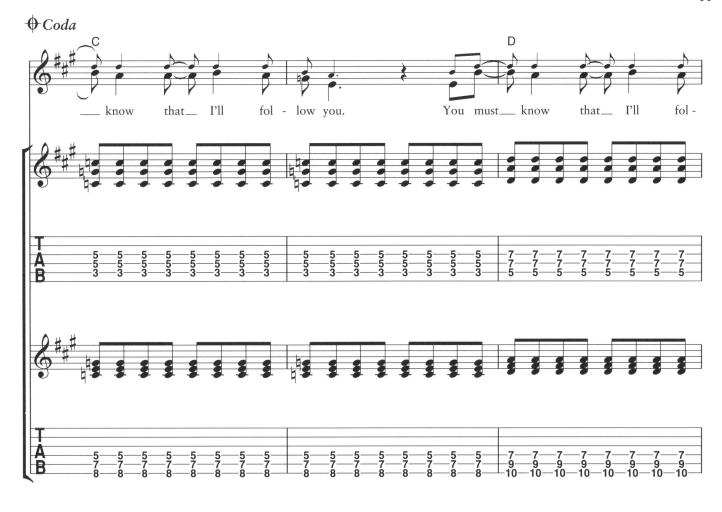

know that I'll fol - low you. You must know that I'll fol -

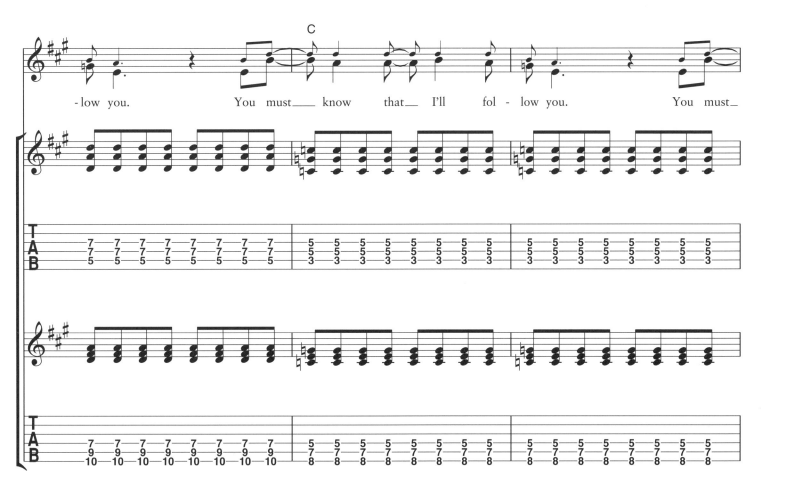

-low you. You must know that I'll fol - low you. You must

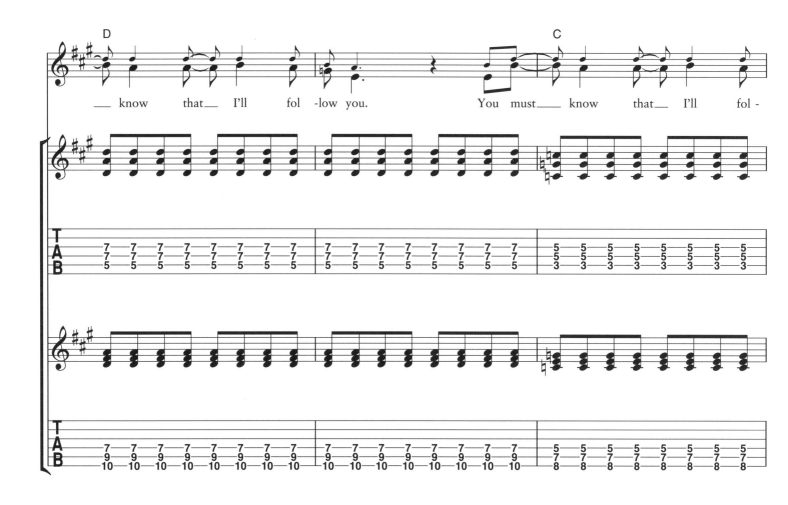

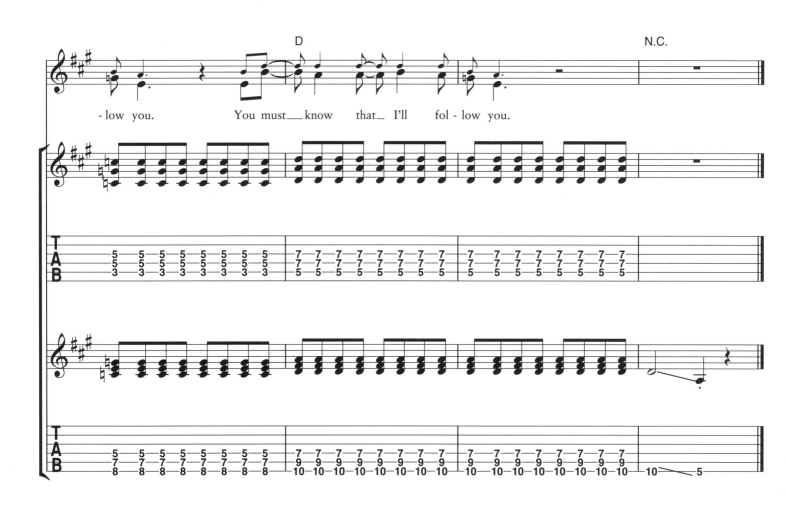

SPITTING GAMES

WORDS AND MUSIC BY GARY LIGHTBODY, JONATHAN QUINN, MARK McCLELLAND AND NATHAN CONNOLLY

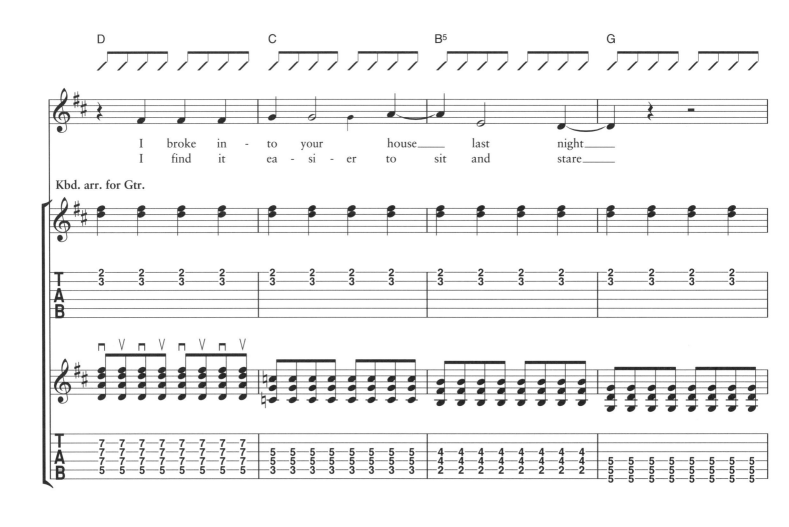

I broke in - to your house____ last night____
I find it ea - si - er to sit and stare____

Kbd. arr. for Gtr.

and left a note at your____ bed - side.____
than push my limbs out to - ward right there.____

38

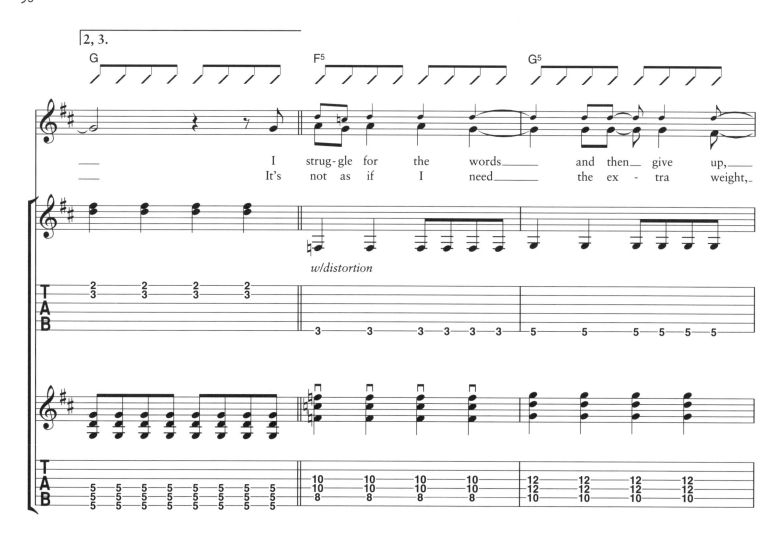

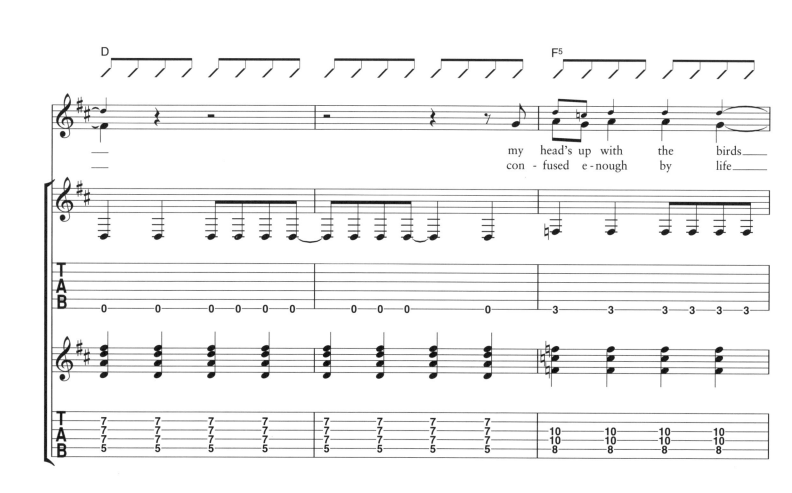

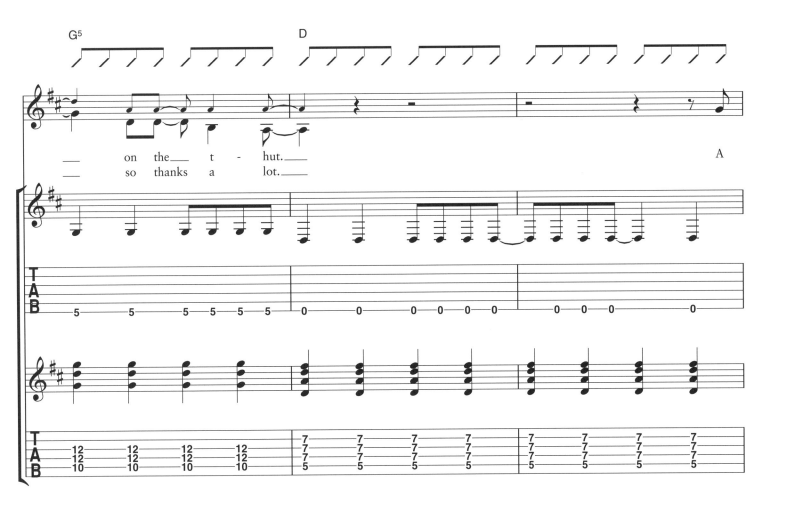

than the plain dis - grace_____ of all___ my let - ters.
raise the roof this once_____ and fol - low me._____

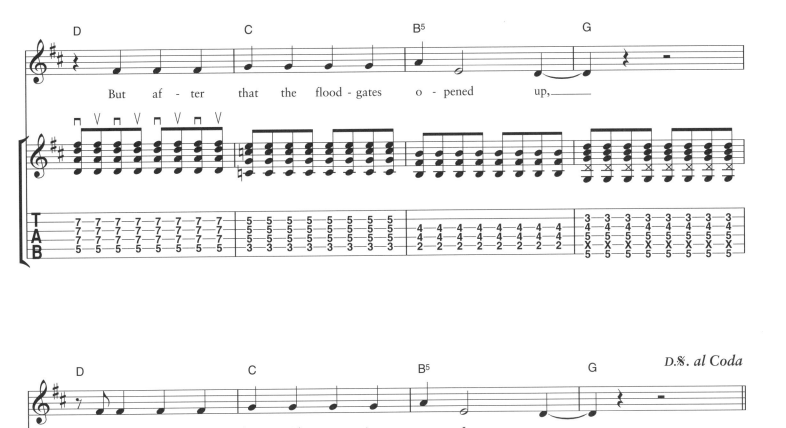

But af - ter that the flood - gates o - pened up,____

D.%. al Coda

and I fell in love with ev - 'ry - one I saw.____

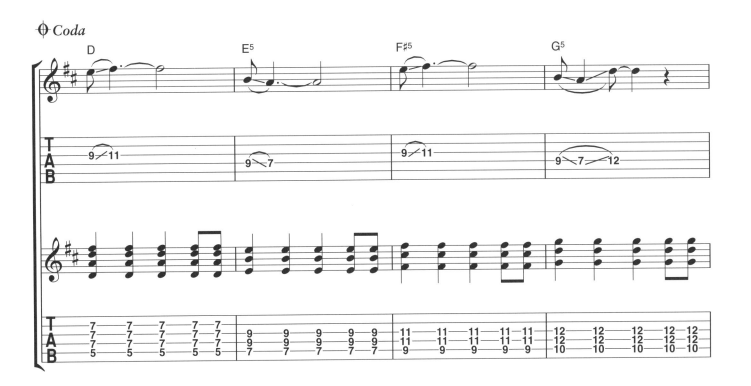

Coda

strug-gle for the words_____ and then_ give up,_____ my

Gtr. 1

w/clean tone

head's up with the birds_____ and I____ see her._____

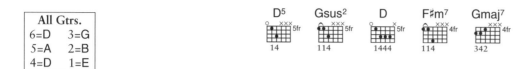

WORDS AND MUSIC BY GARY LIGHTBODY, JONATHAN QUINN, MARK McCLELLAND AND NATHAN CONNOLLY

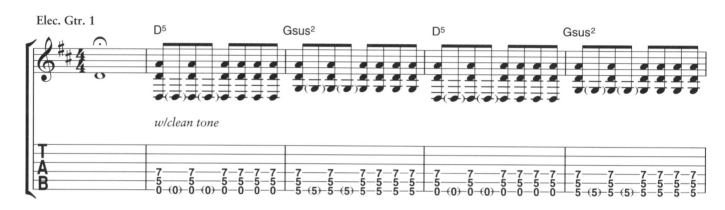

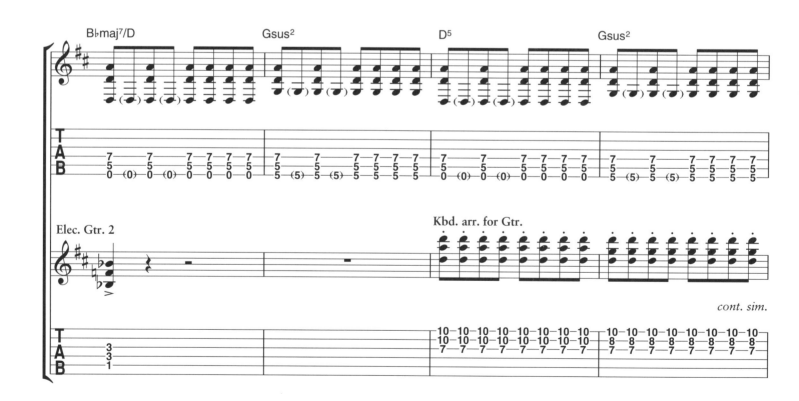

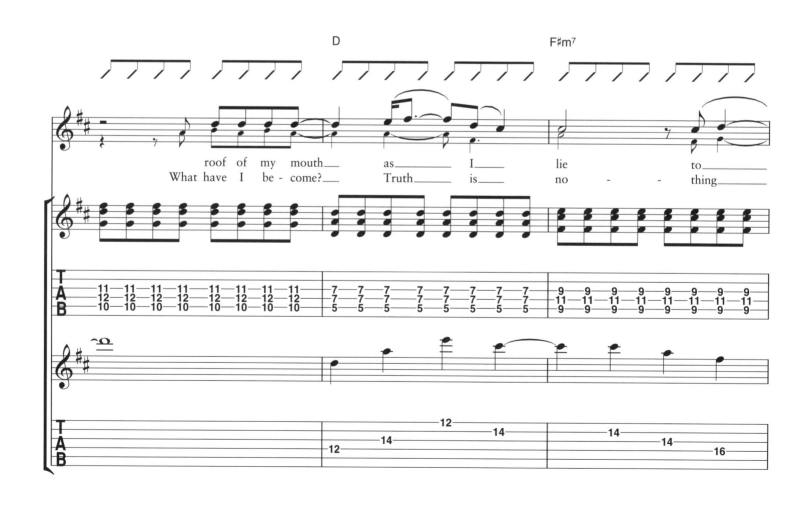

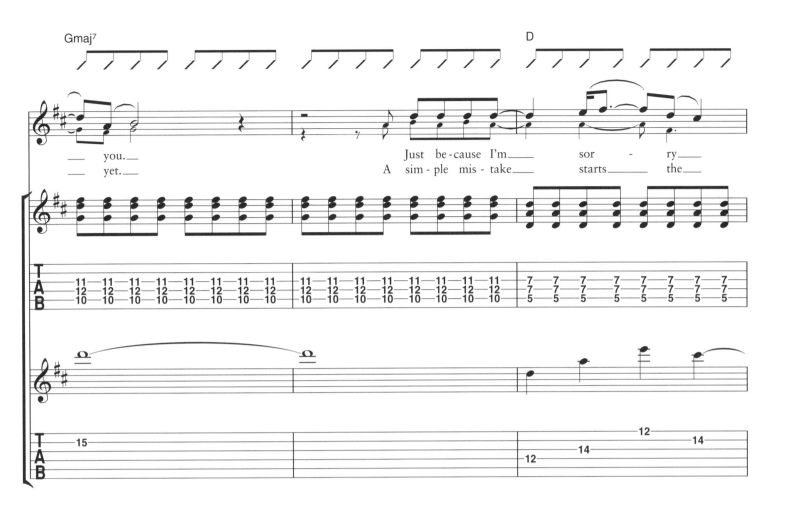

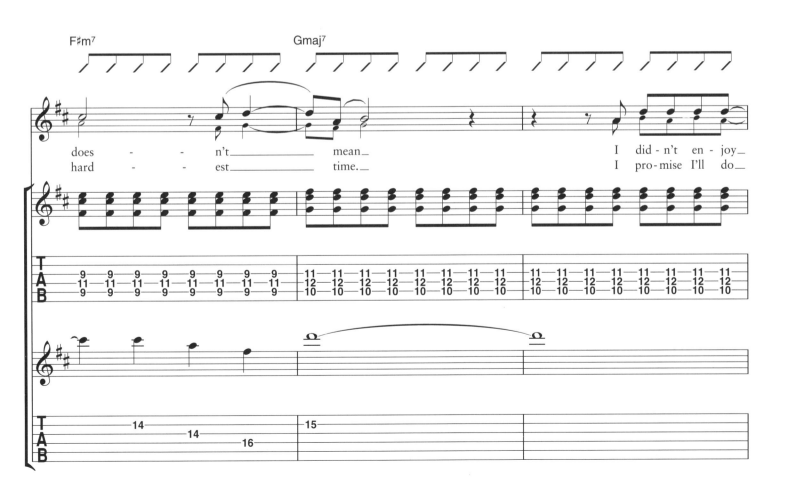

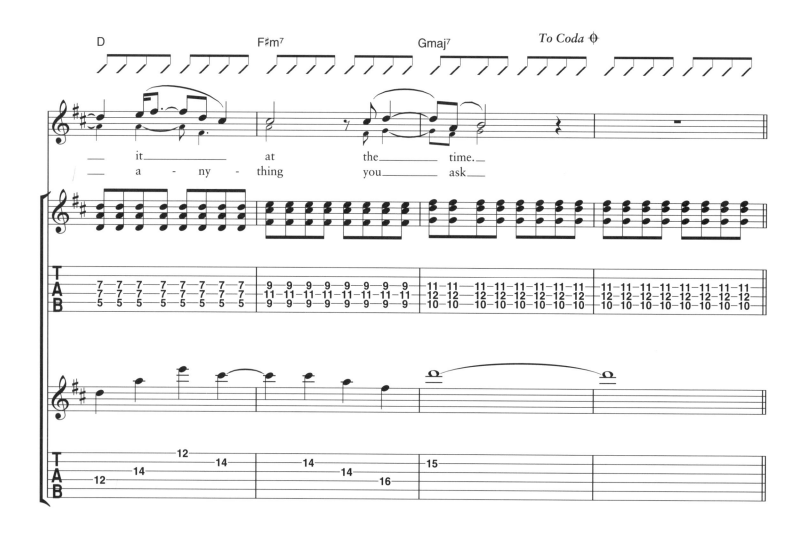

it _____ at the _____ time.
a - ny - thing you _____ ask _____

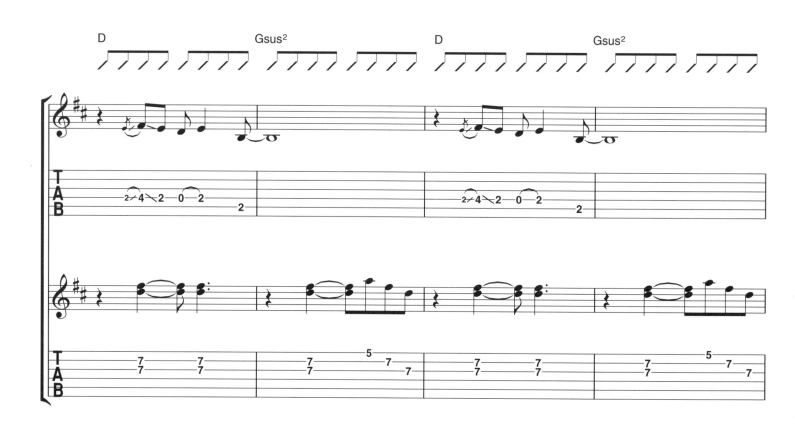

Verse 3:
You're the only thing that I love
It scares me more every day
On my knees I think clearer.

Verse 4:
Goodness knows I saw it coming
Or at least I'll claim I did
But in truth I'm lost for words.

RUN

WORDS AND MUSIC BY GARY LIGHTBODY, JONATHAN QUINN, MARK McCLELLAND, NATHAN CONNOLLY AND IAIN ARCHER

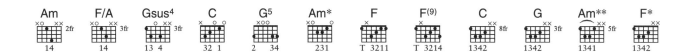

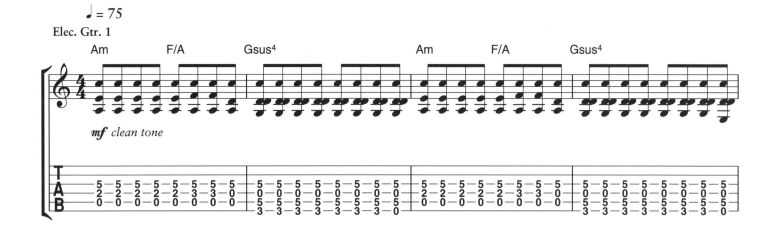

1. I'll sing it

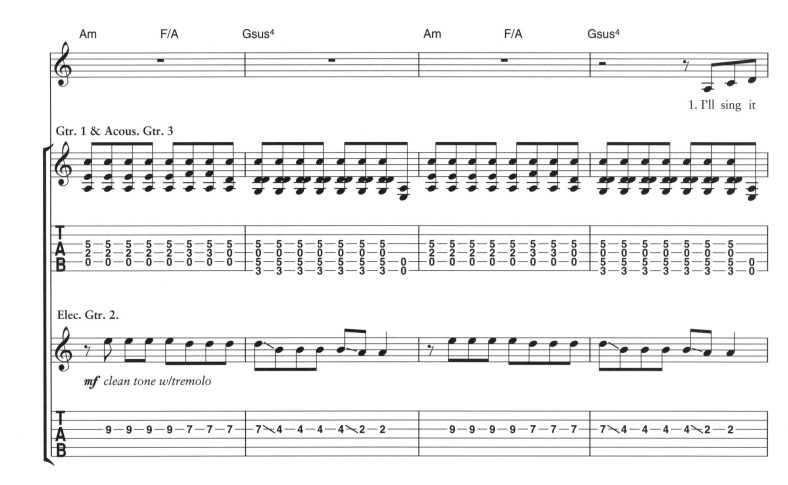

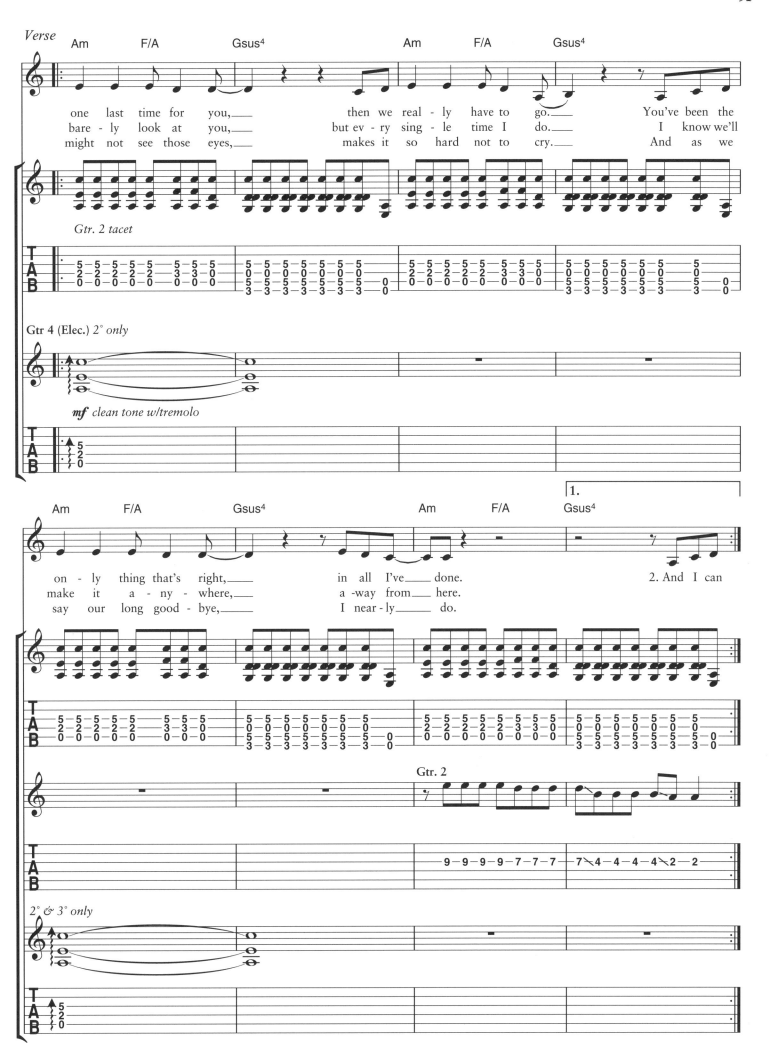

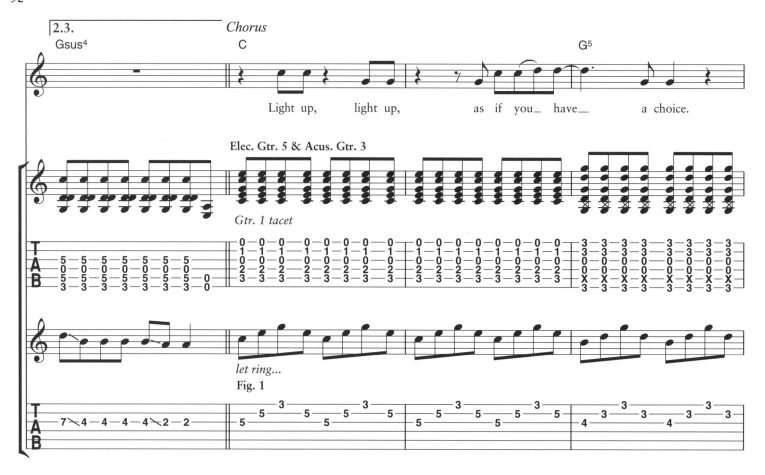

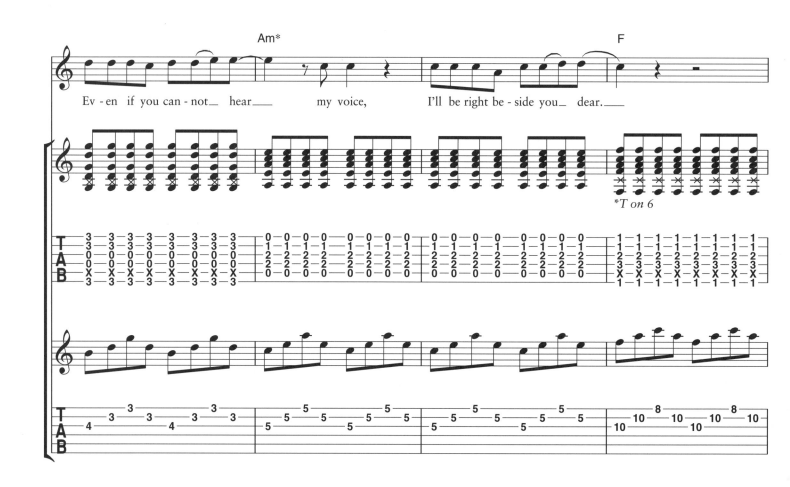

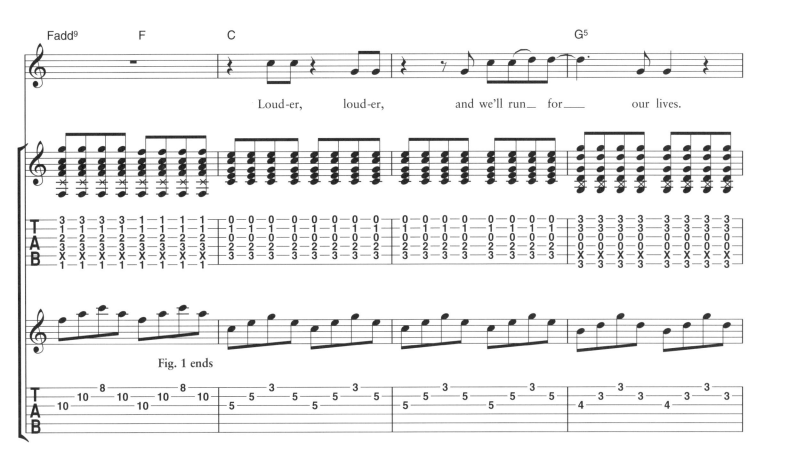

Loud-er,   loud-er,   and we'll run__ for__   our lives.

Fig. 1 ends

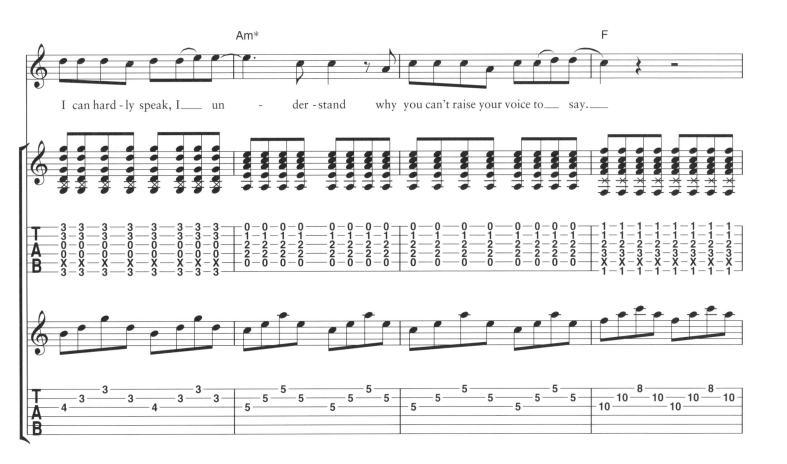

I can hard-ly speak, I__ un - der-stand   why you can't raise your voice to__ say.__

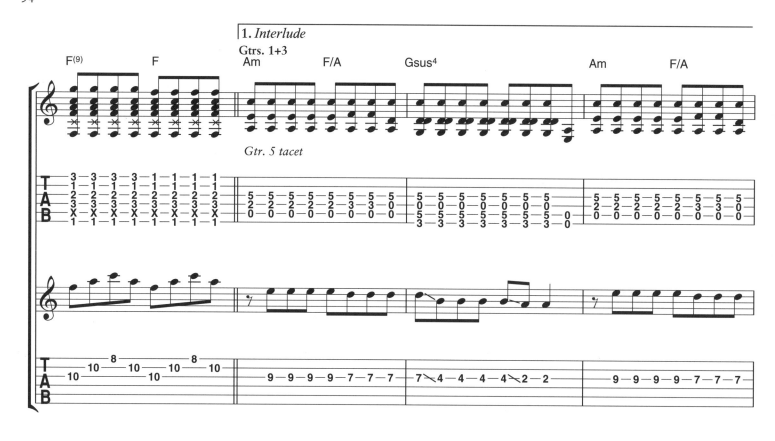

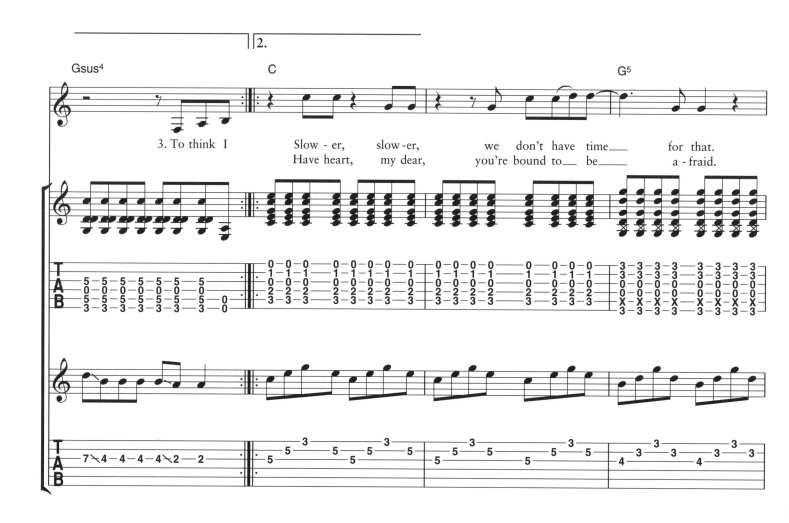

3. To think I

Slow - er, slow -er, we don't have time___ for that.
Have heart, my dear, you're bound to___ be___ a - fraid.

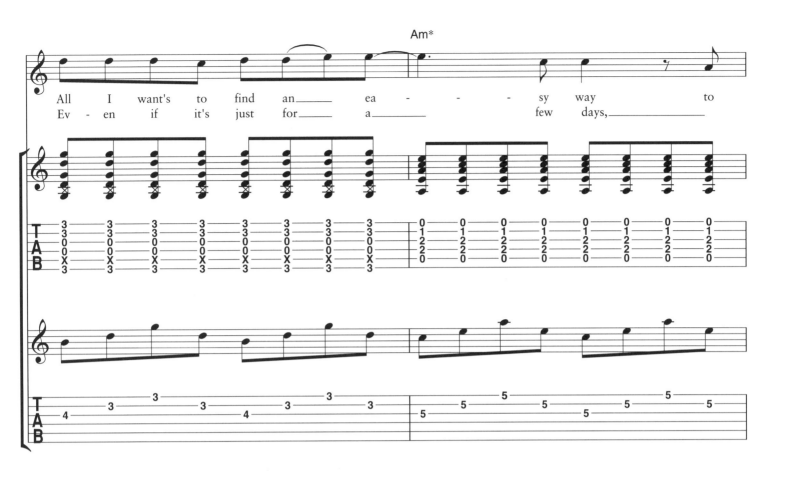

All   I   want's   to   find   an____   ea - - - sy   way   to
Ev - en   if   it's   just   for____   a_____   few   days,_____

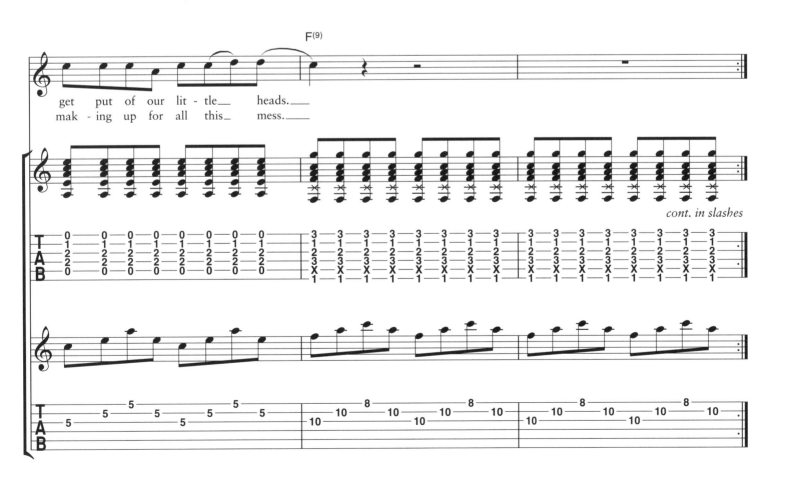

get   put   of   our   lit - tle___   heads.___
mak - ing   up   for   all   this___   mess.___

cont. in slashes

Chorus

GRAZED KNEES

WORDS AND MUSIC BY GARY LIGHTBODY, JONATHAN QUINN, MARK McCLELLAND AND NATHAN CONNOLLY

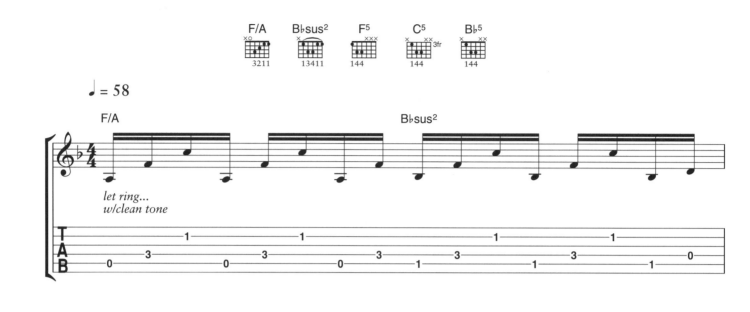

I'm try - ing not to__ stare,   it's too
ea - si - er to__ lie__   and be

__ late.__   The blan - ket's o - ver__ there   if you
__ safe,__   time__ and time a - gain__   I'm half

60

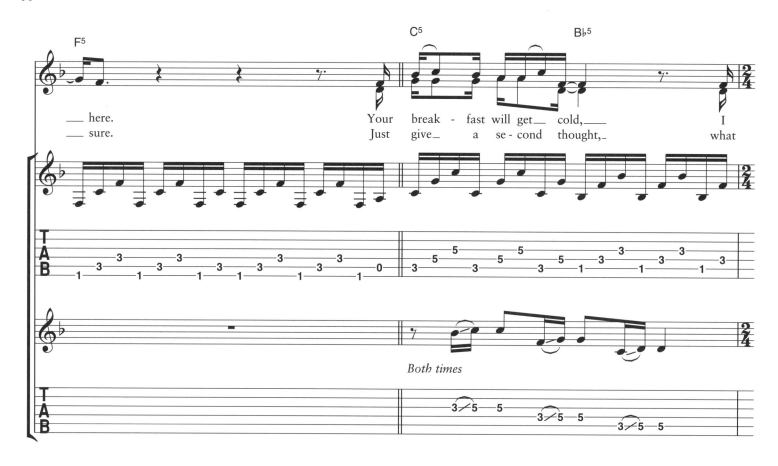

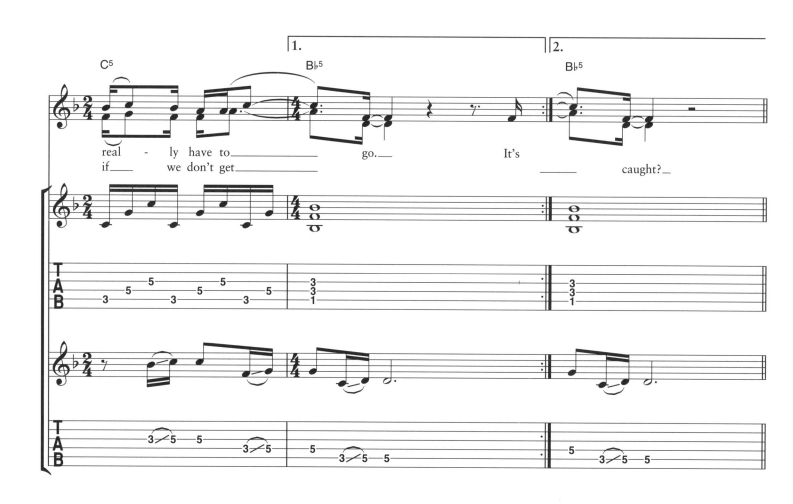

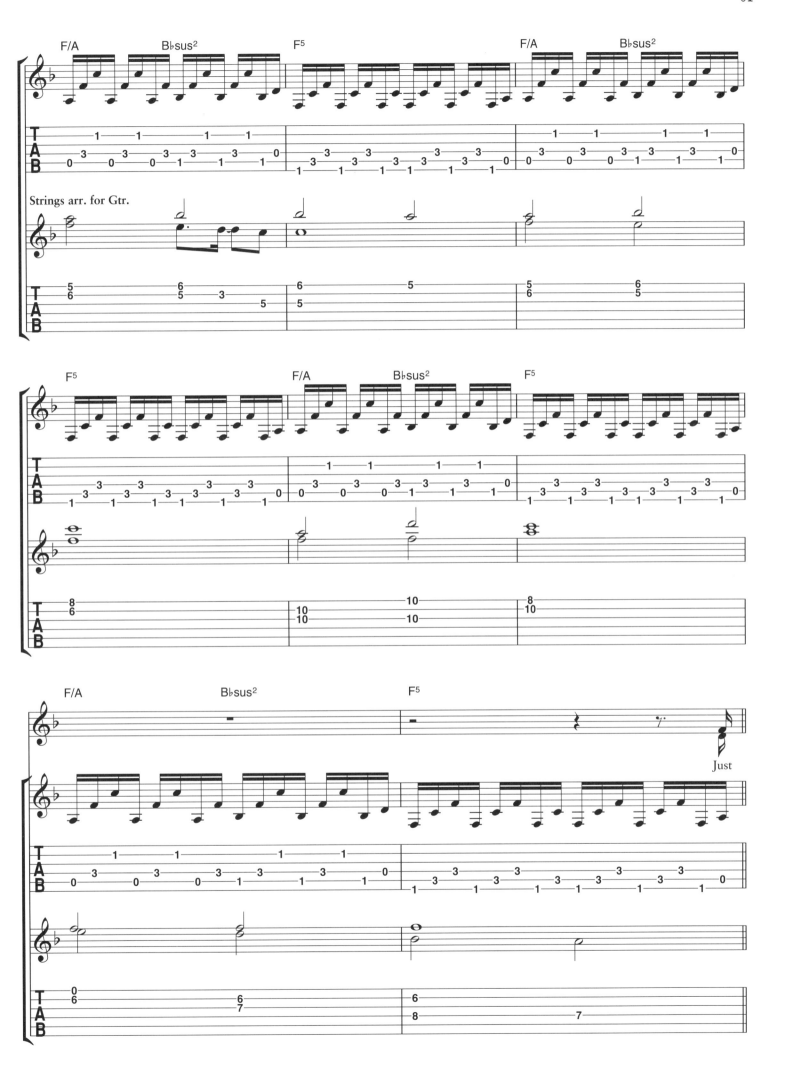

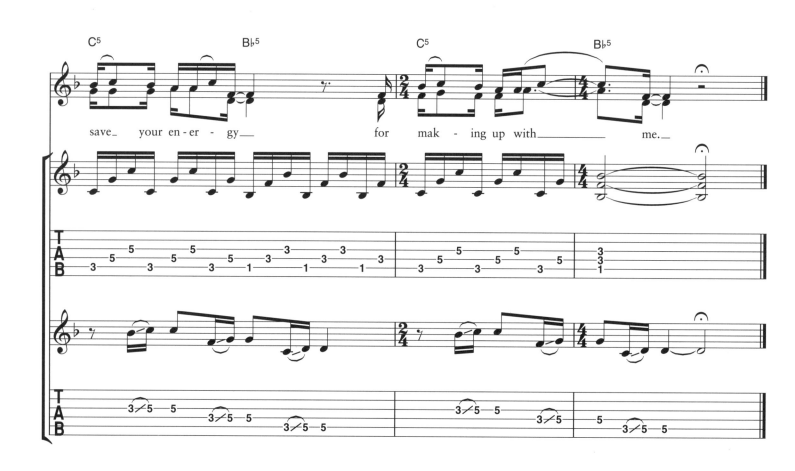

WAYS & MEANS

WORDS AND MUSIC BY GARY LIGHTBODY, JONATHAN QUINN, MARK McCLELLAND AND IAIN ARCHER

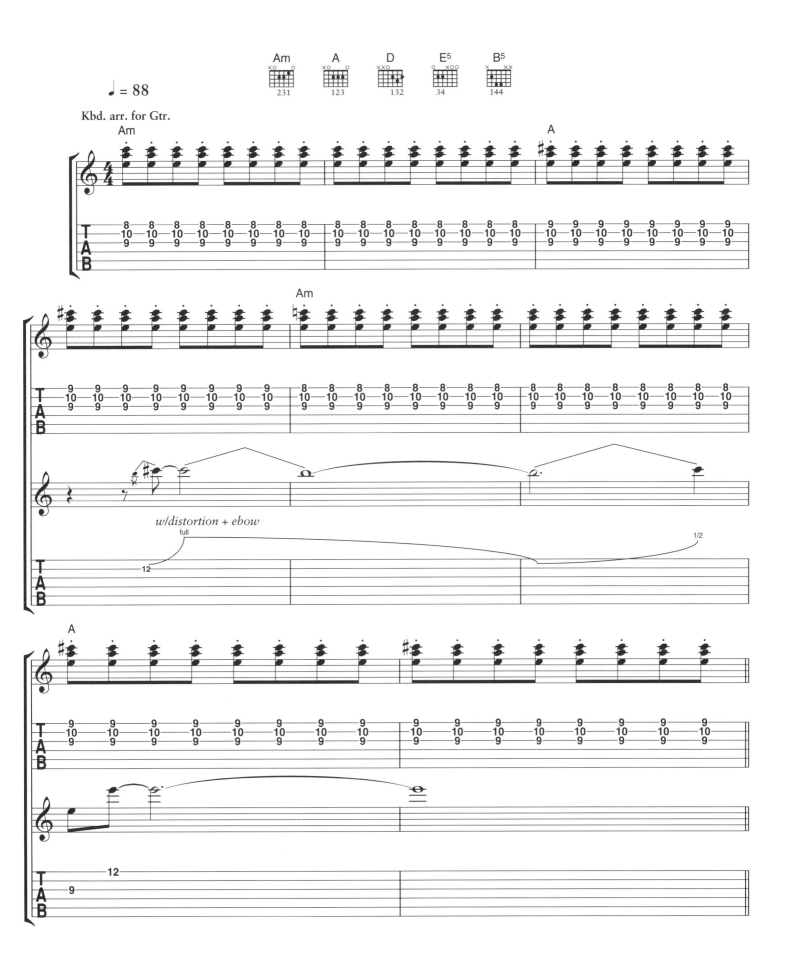

Kbd. arr. for Gtr.

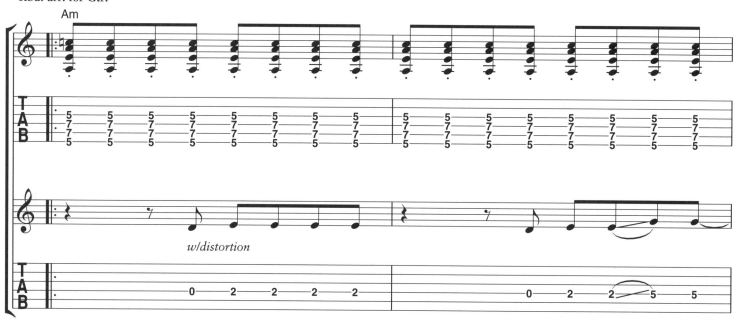

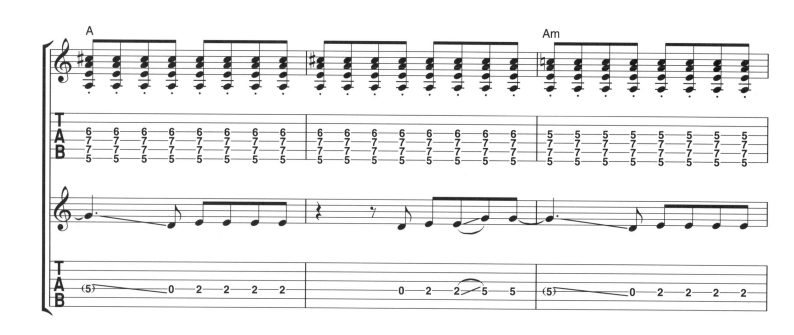

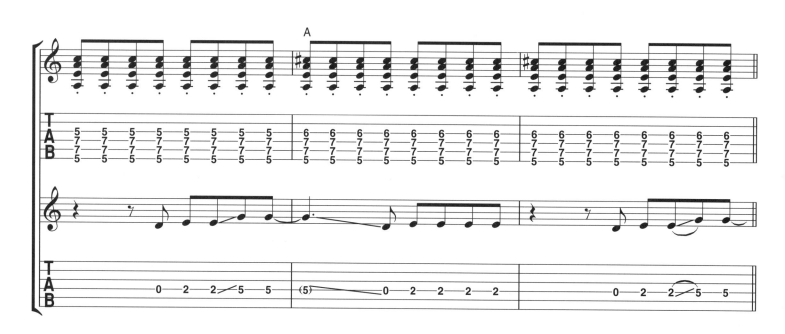

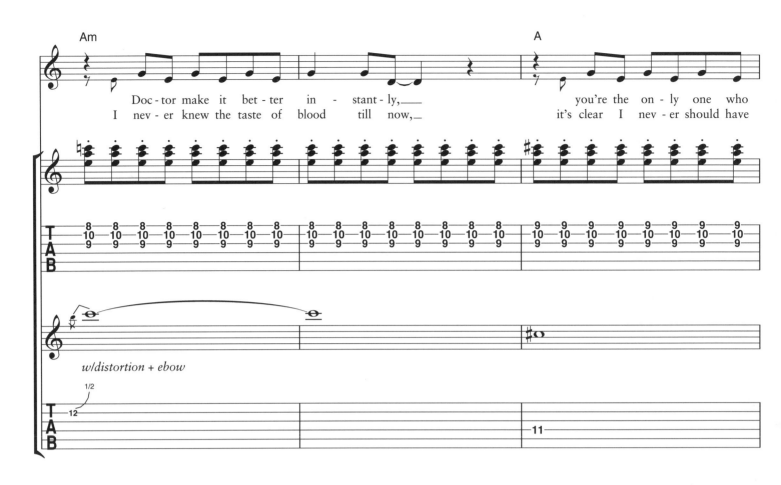

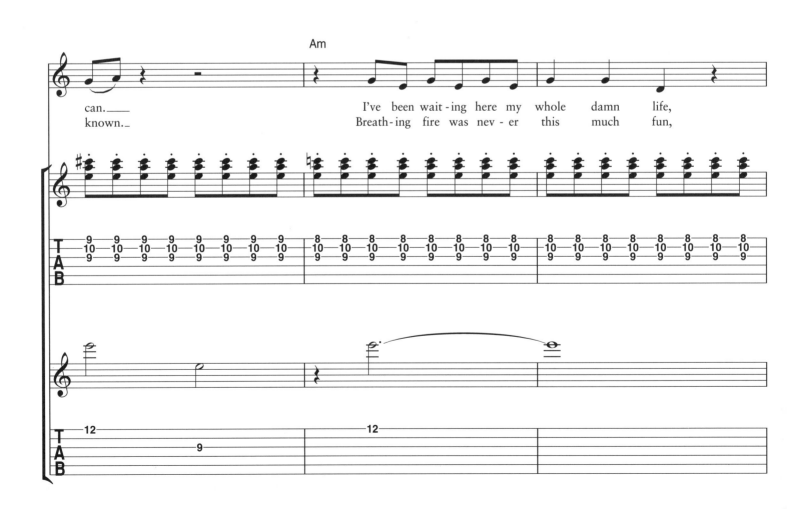

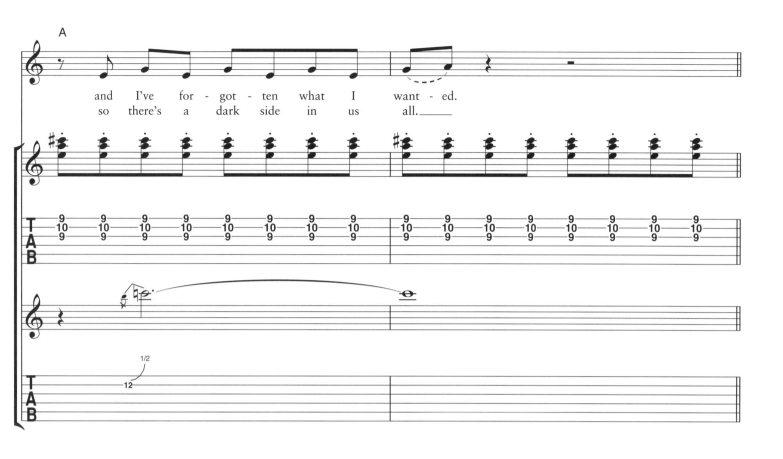

and I've for - got - ten what I want - ed.
so there's a dark side in us all.____

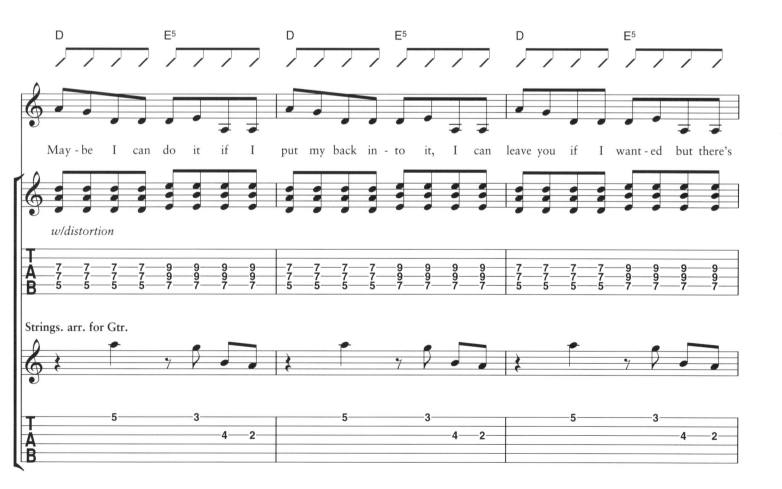

May - be I can do it if I put my back in - to it, I can leave you if I want - ed but there's

w/distortion

Strings. arr. for Gtr.

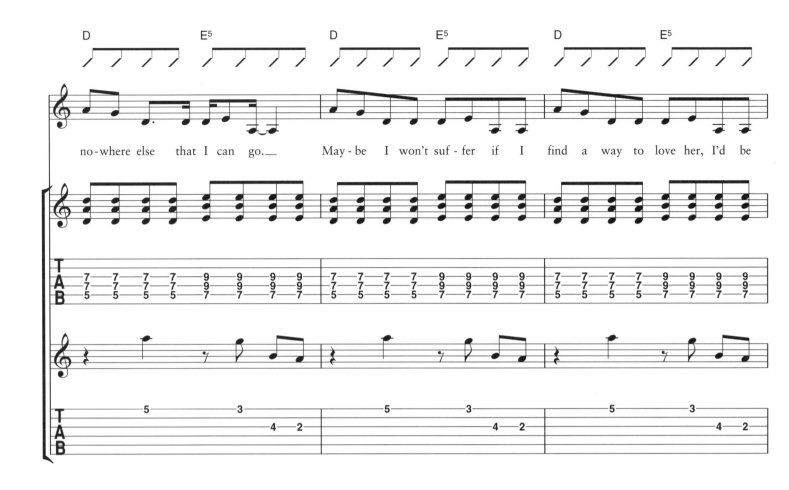

no-where else that I can go.__ May-be I won't suf-fer if I find a way to love her, I'd be

ly-ing to my-self, but there is no way out that I can see.__

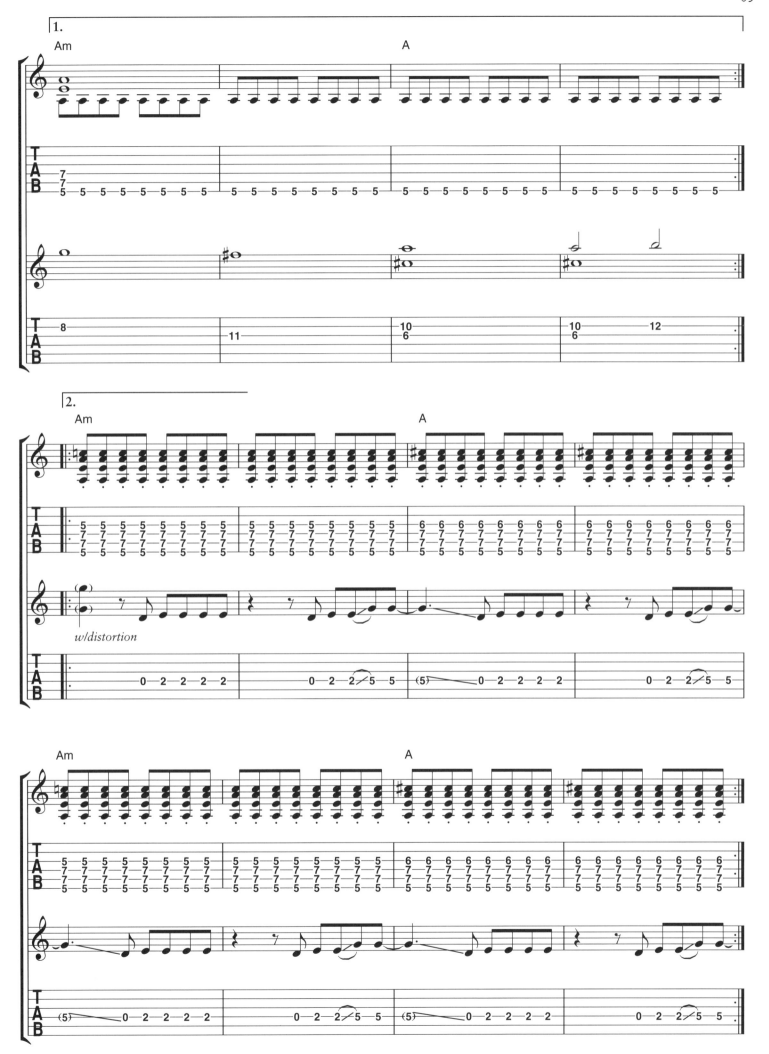

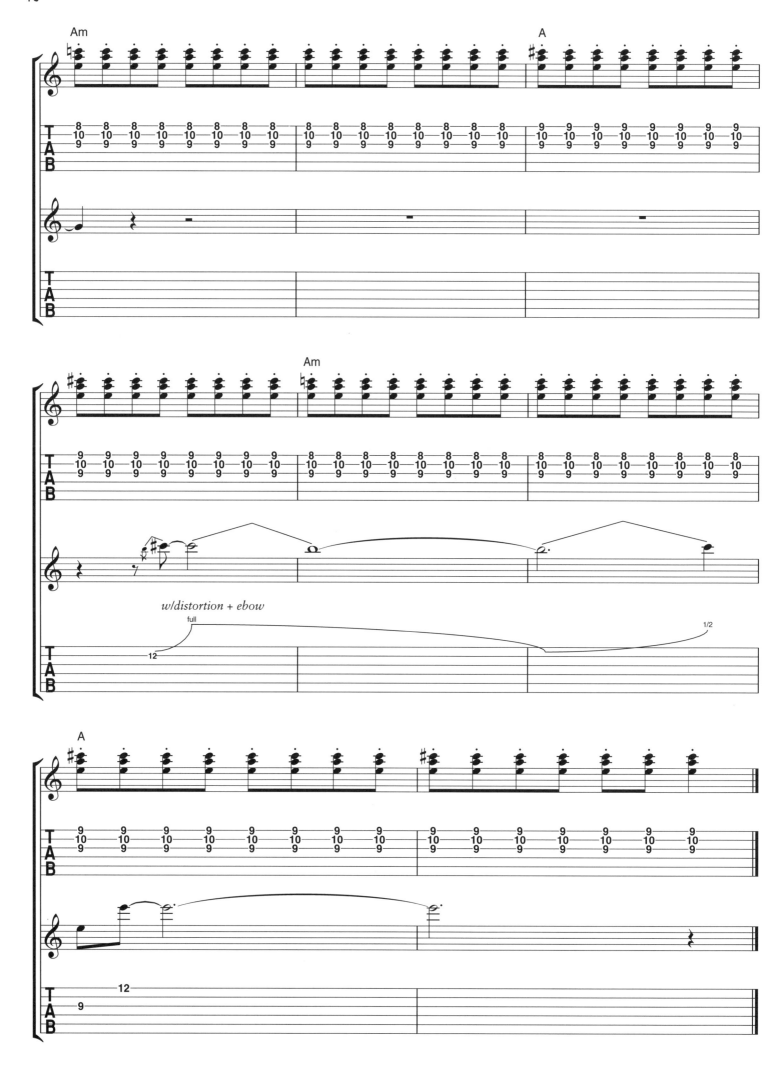

TINY LITTLE FRACTURES

WORDS AND MUSIC BY GARY LIGHTBODY, JONATHAN QUINN, MARK McCLELLAND AND NATHAN CONNOLLY

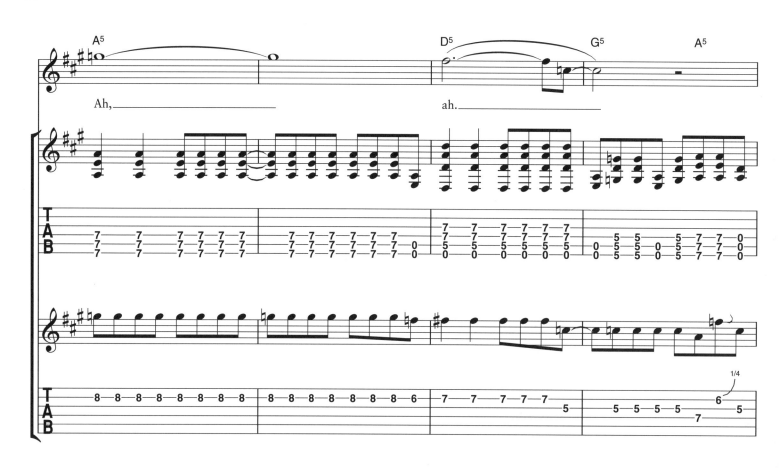

Ah,_____ ah._____

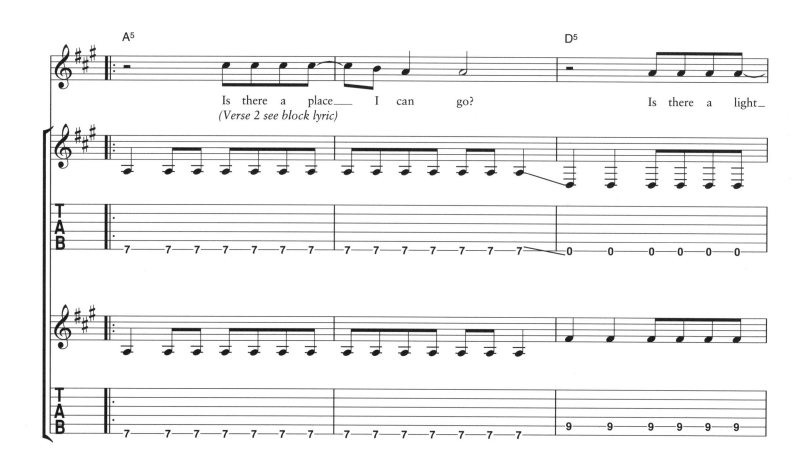

Is there a place___ I can go?
(Verse 2 see block lyric)

Is there a light_

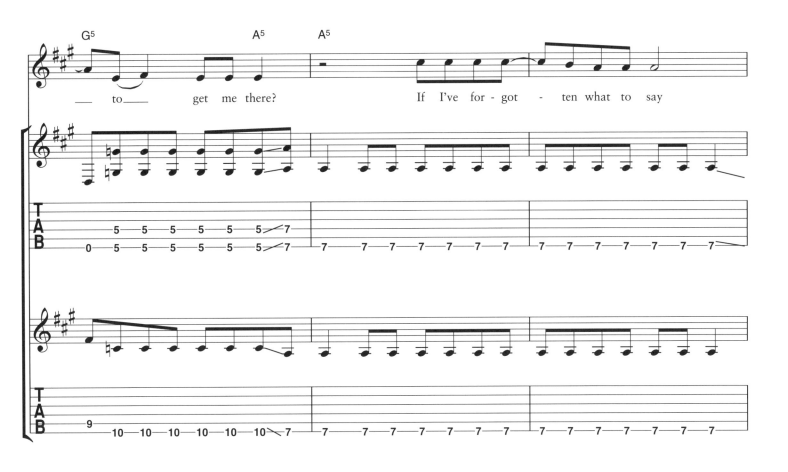

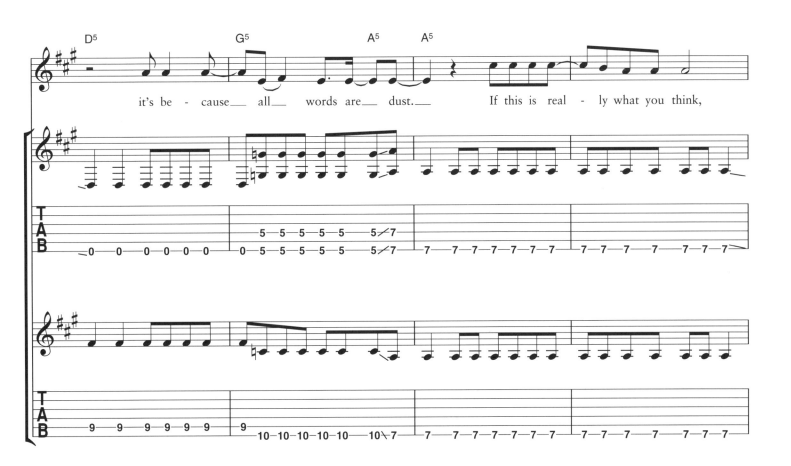

74

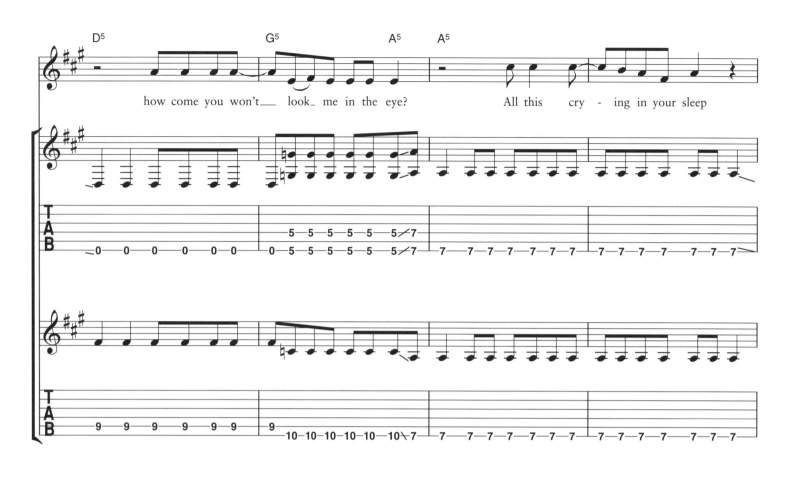

how come you won't___ look___ me in the eye?   All this   cry - ing in your sleep

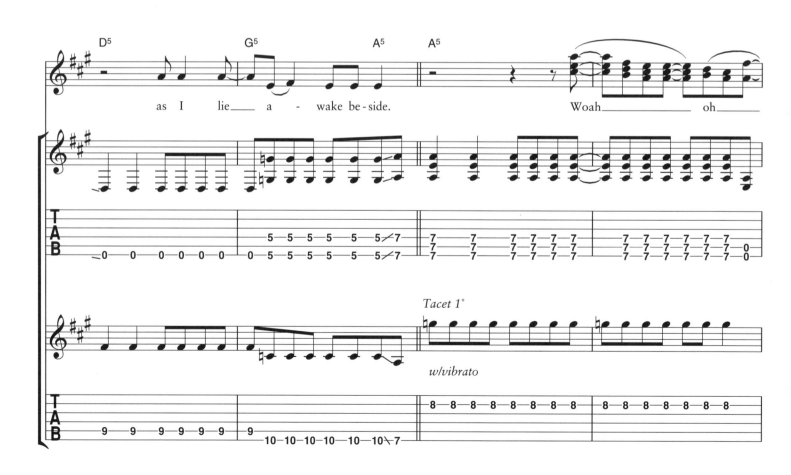

as I lie___ a - wake be - side.   Woah_____ oh_____

Tacet 1°

w/vibrato

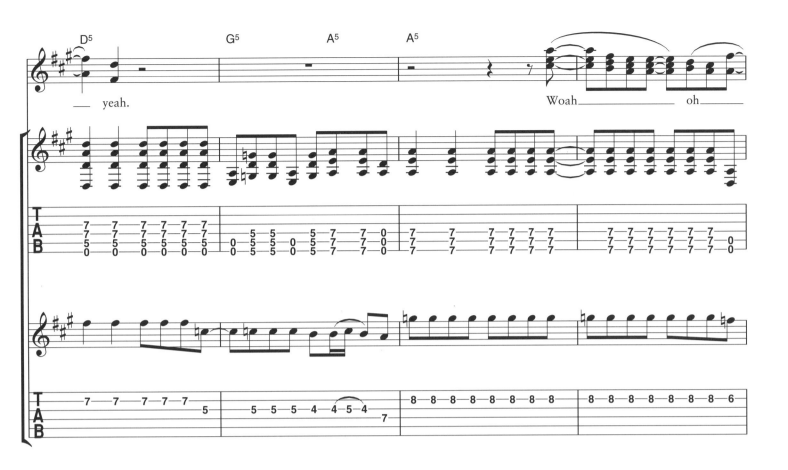

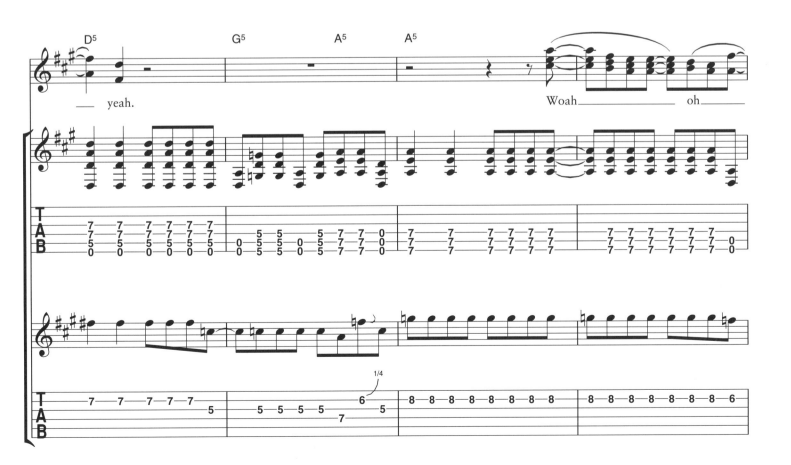

Verse 2:
Is there a T-shirt I can wear?
'Cause I am soaking look at me
What do you mean I don't love you?
I am standing here, aren't I?
Maybe you thought of it first
Maybe I get all the praise
Is there a place I can go?
Is there a light to get me there?

SOMEWHERE A CLOCK IS TICKING

WORDS AND MUSIC BY GARY LIGHTBODY, JONATHAN QUINN, MARK McCLELLAND AND IAIN ARCHER

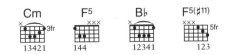

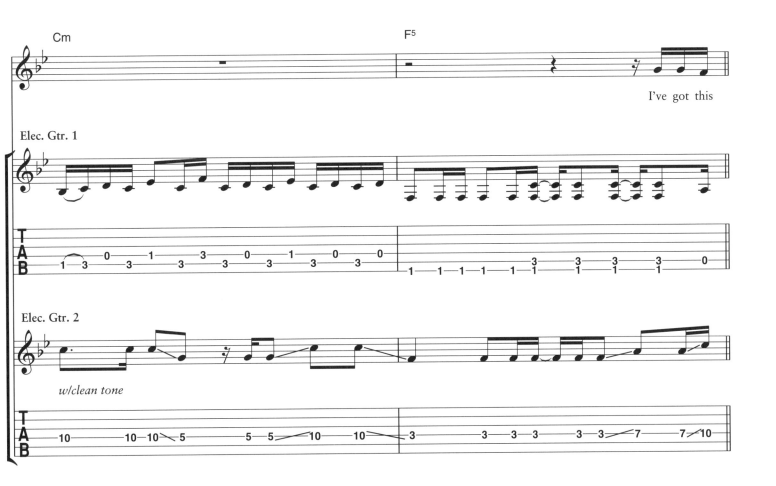

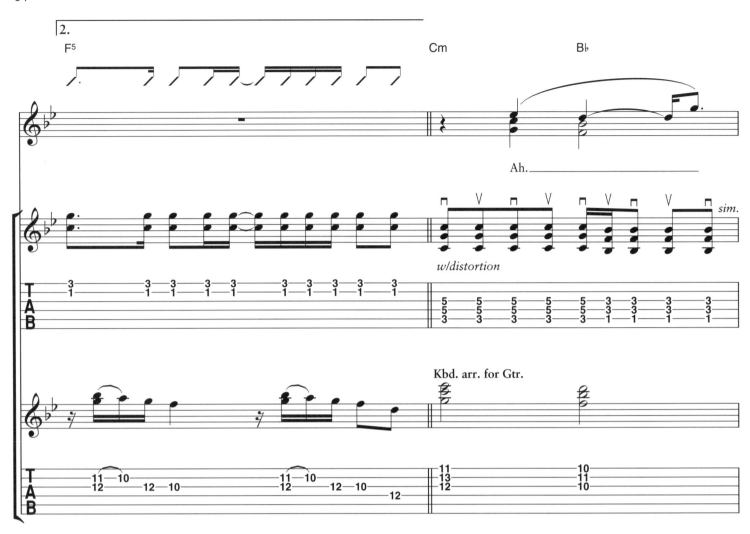

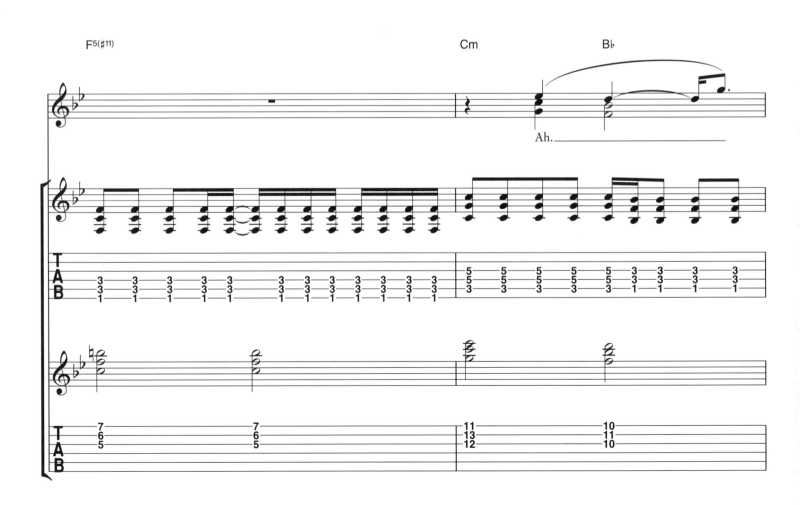

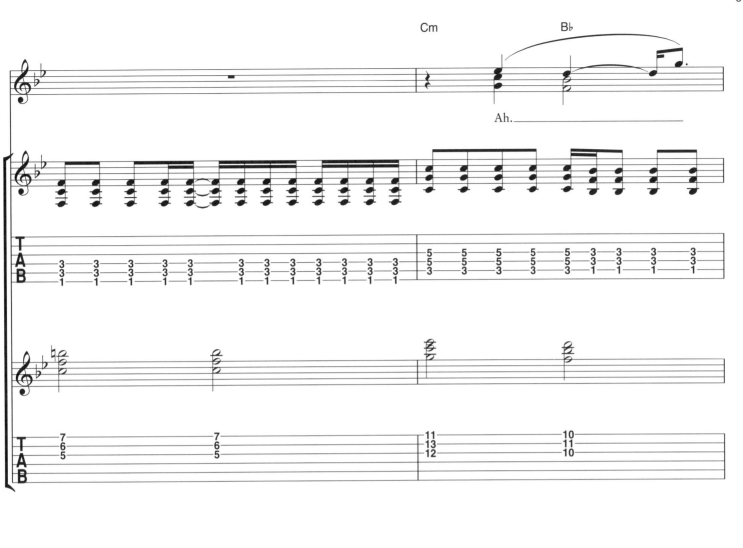

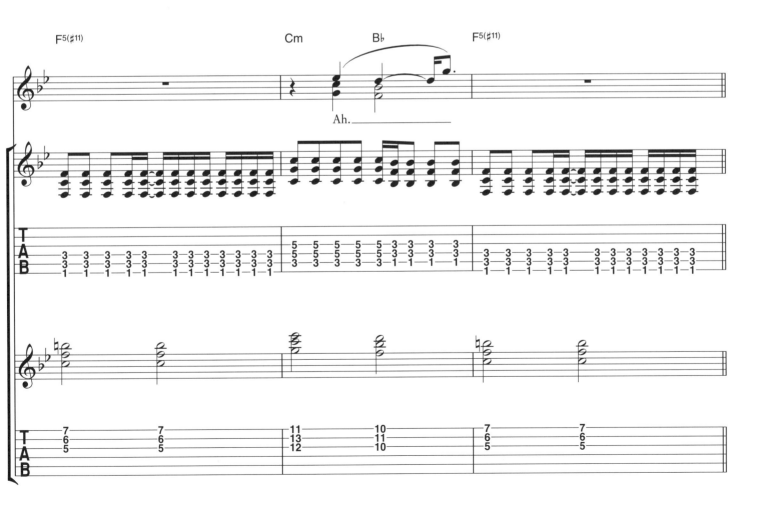

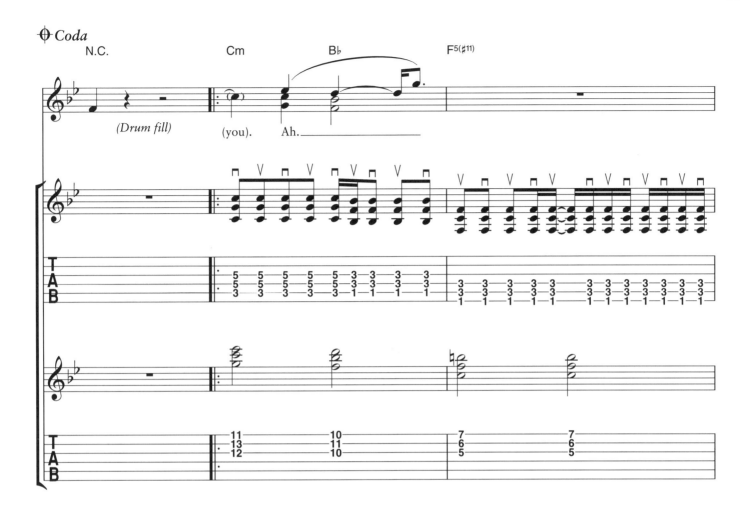

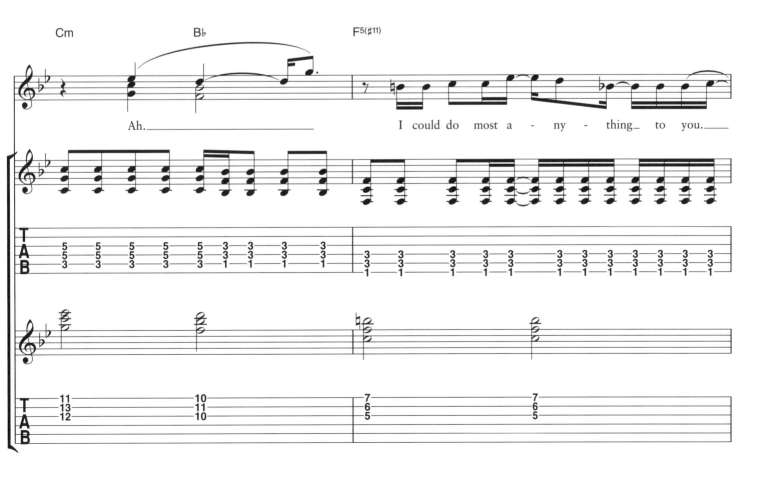

I could do most a - ny - thing_ to you._

w/clean tone

Kbd. arr. for Gtr.

SAME

WORDS AND MUSIC BY GARY LIGHTBODY, JONATHAN QUINN, MARK McCLELLAND AND NATHAN CONNOLLY

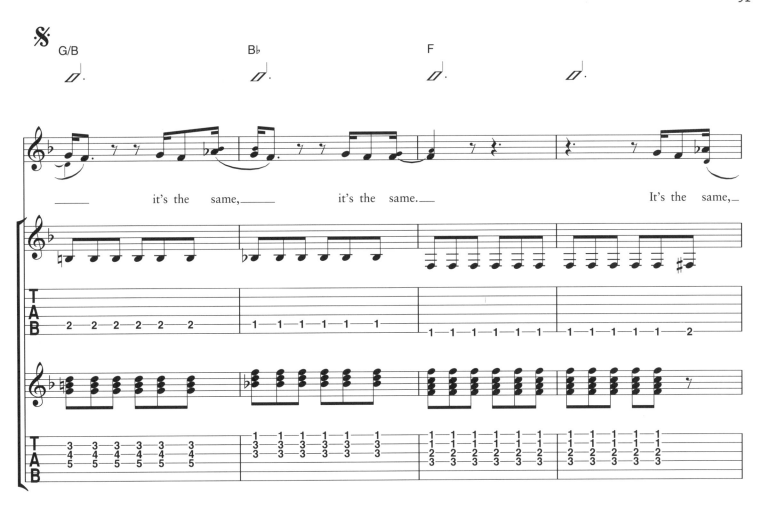

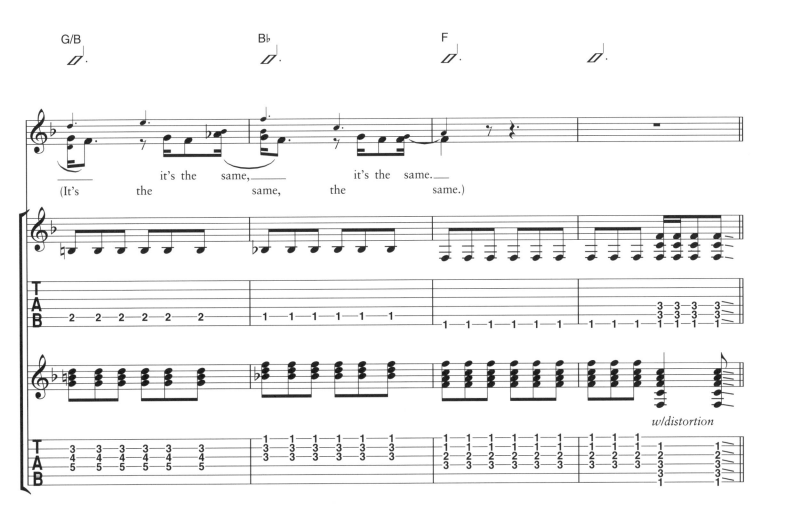

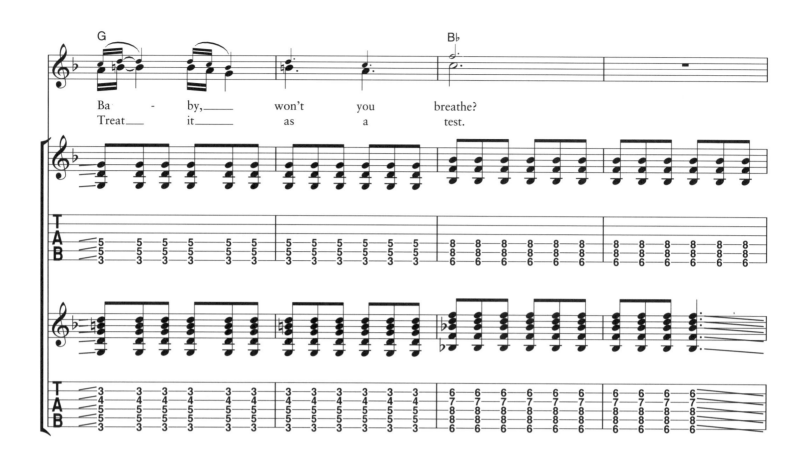

Ba - by,___ won't you breathe?
Treat___ it___ as a test.

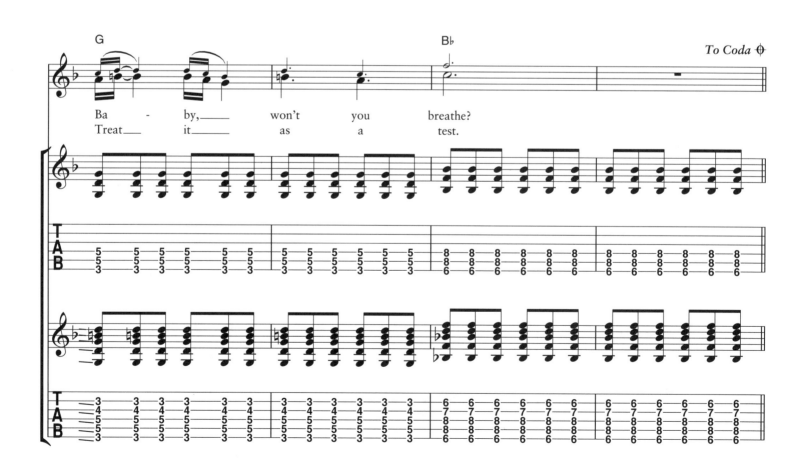

Ba - by,___ won't you breathe?
Treat___ it___ as a test.

To Coda ⊕

clear heart of her appears, eyes, me shiver on the seats. It's the same,

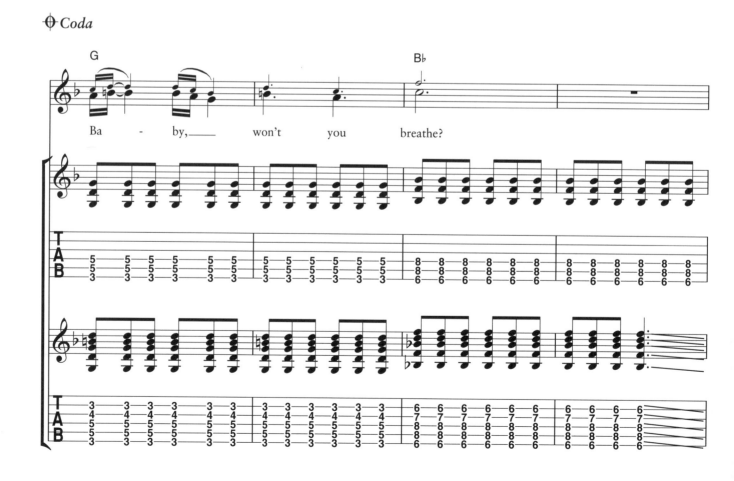

Baby, won't you breathe?

WE CAN RUN AWAY NOW THEY'RE ALL DEAD AND GONE

WORDS AND MUSIC BY GARY LIGHTBODY, JONATHAN QUINN AND MARK McCLELLAND

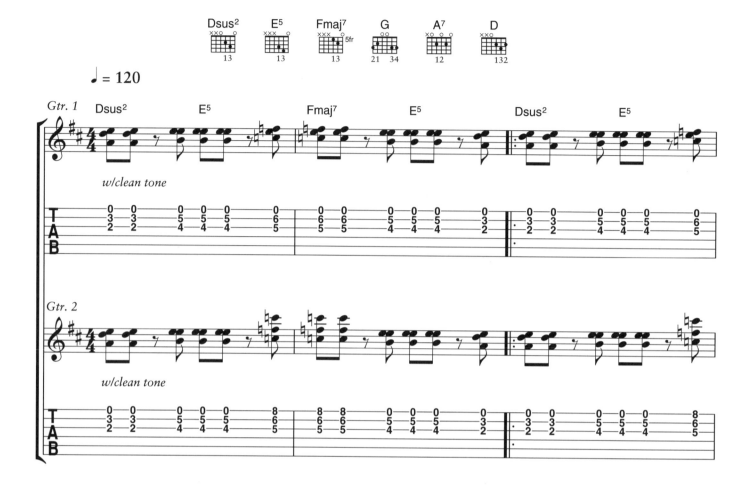

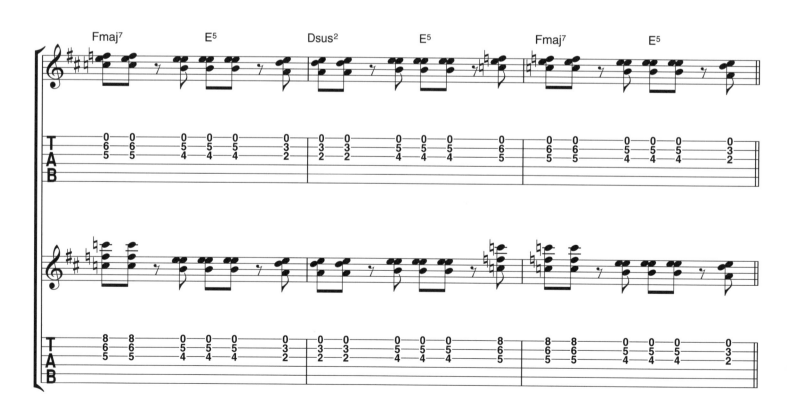

Verse

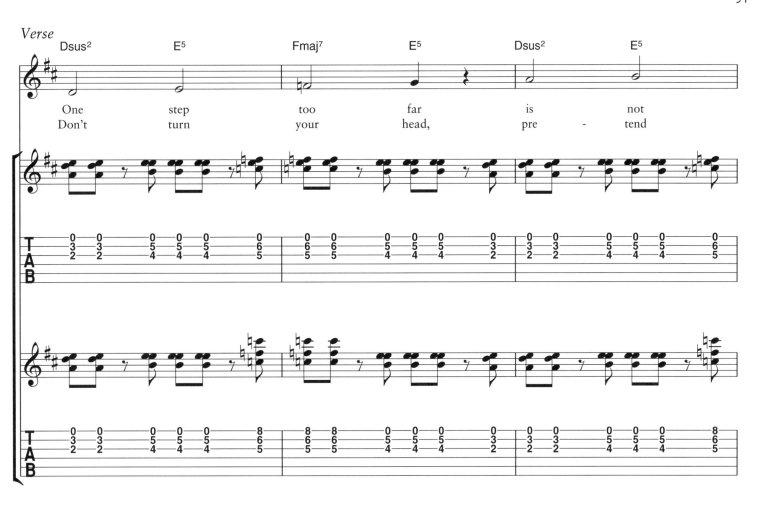

One step too far is not
Don't turn your head, pre - tend

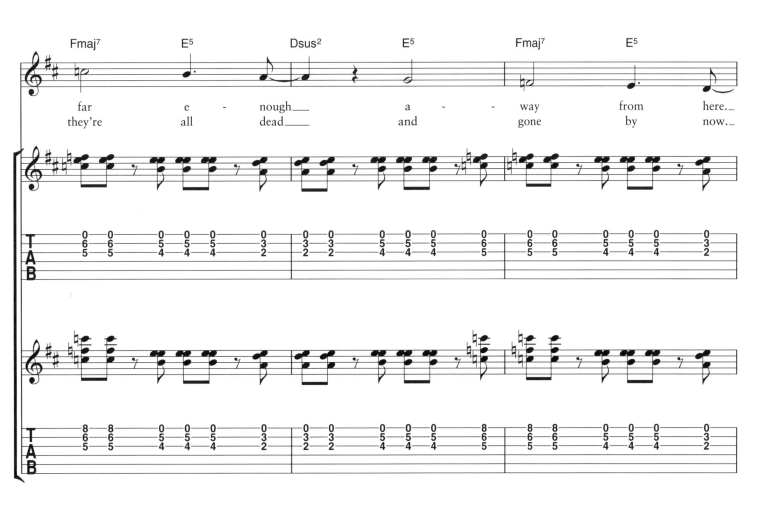

far e - nough a - way from here.
they're all dead and gone by now.

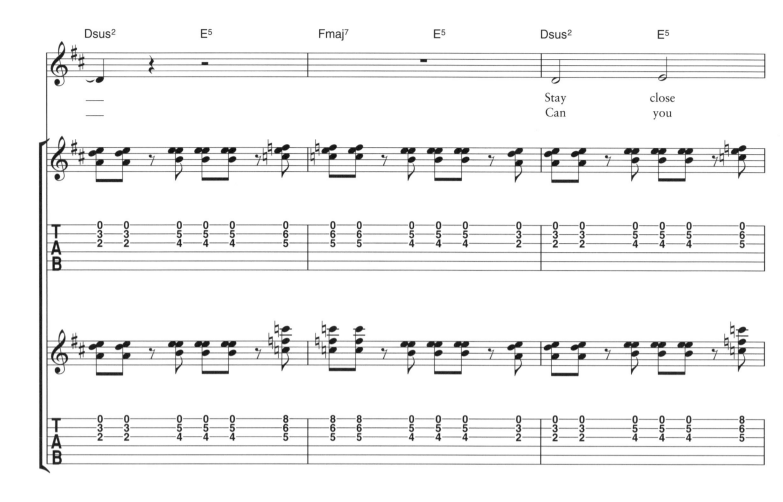

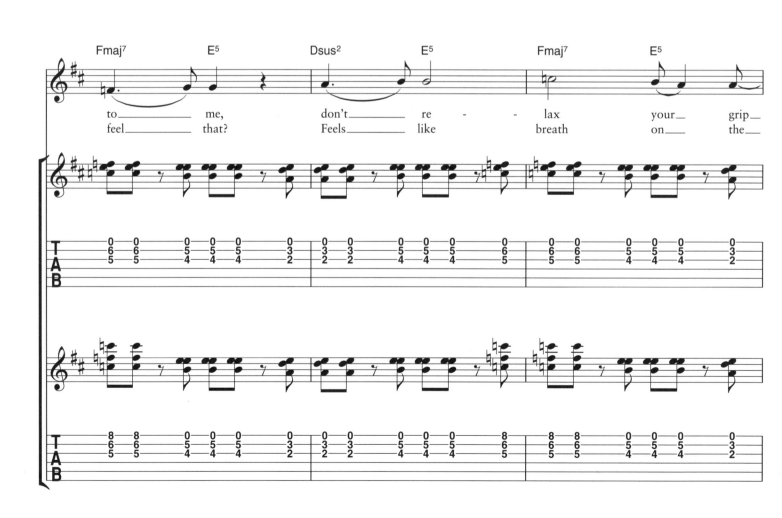

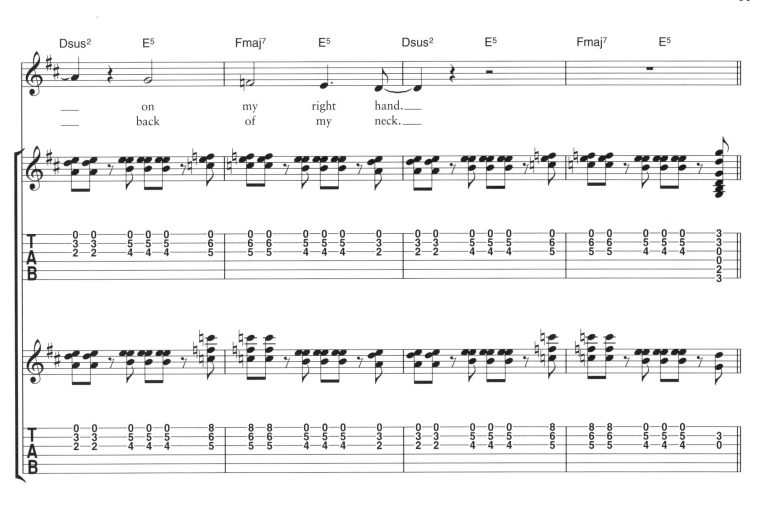

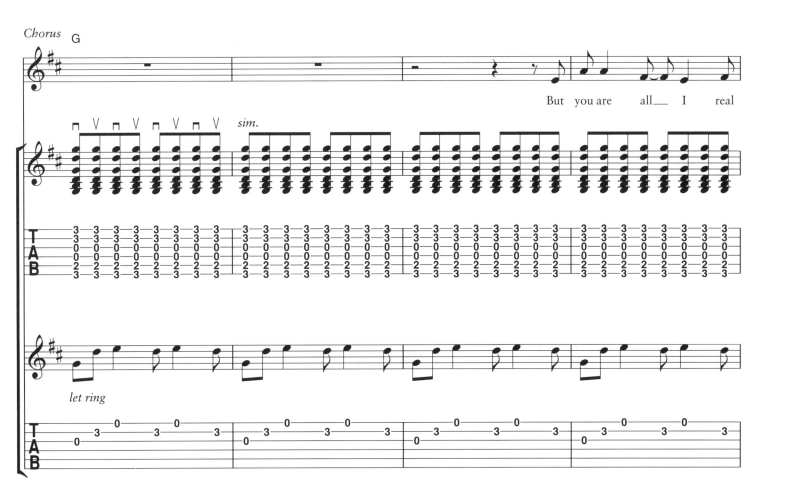

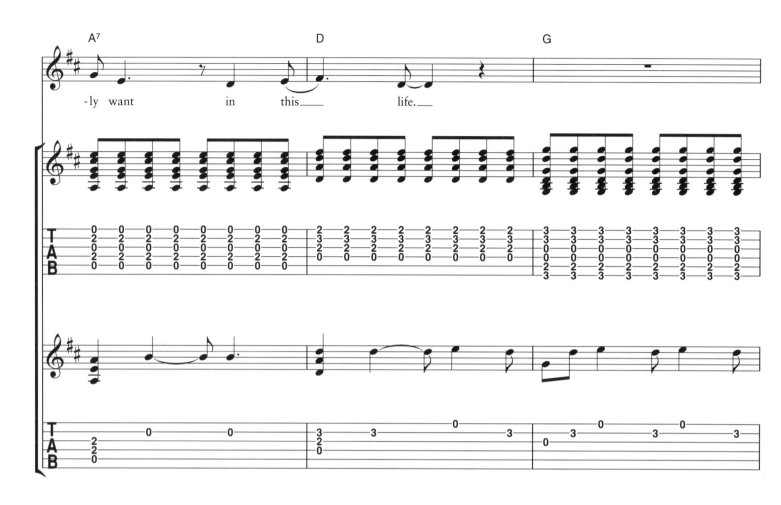

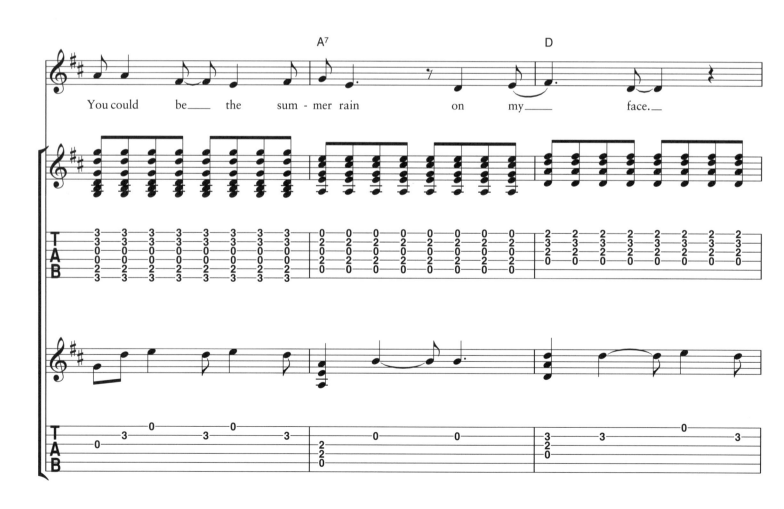

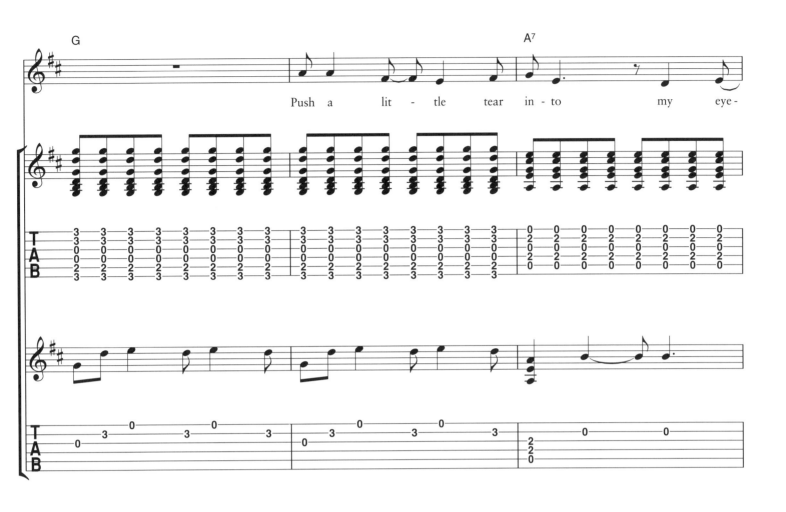

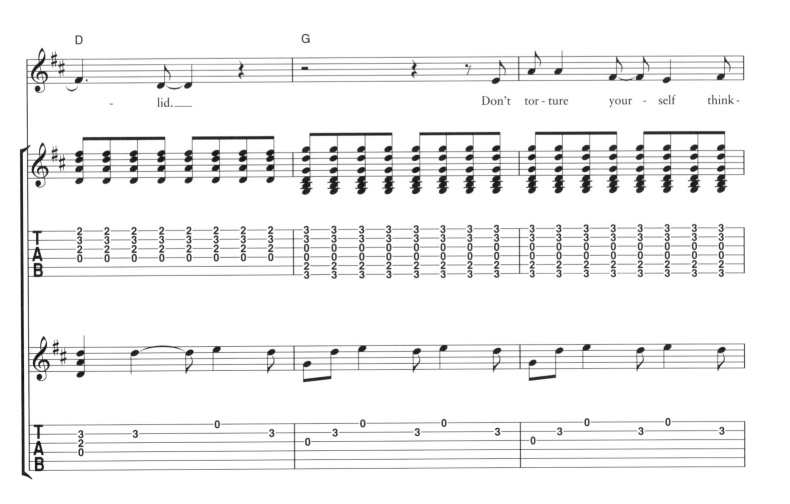

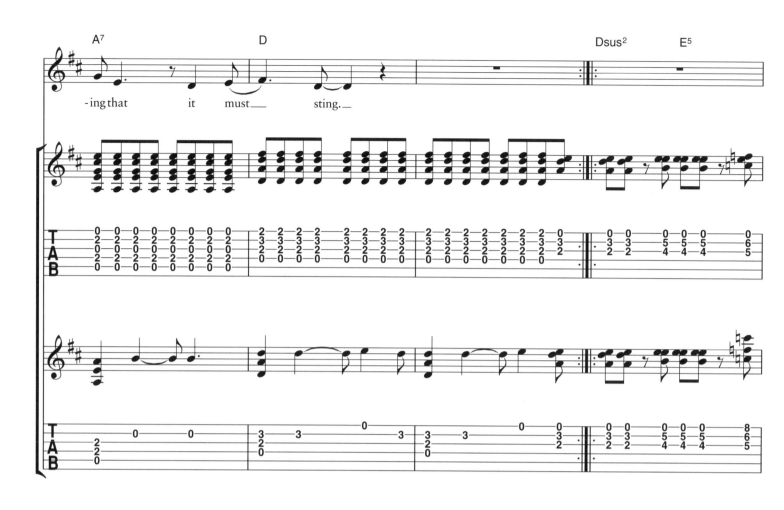

-ing that it must___ sting.___

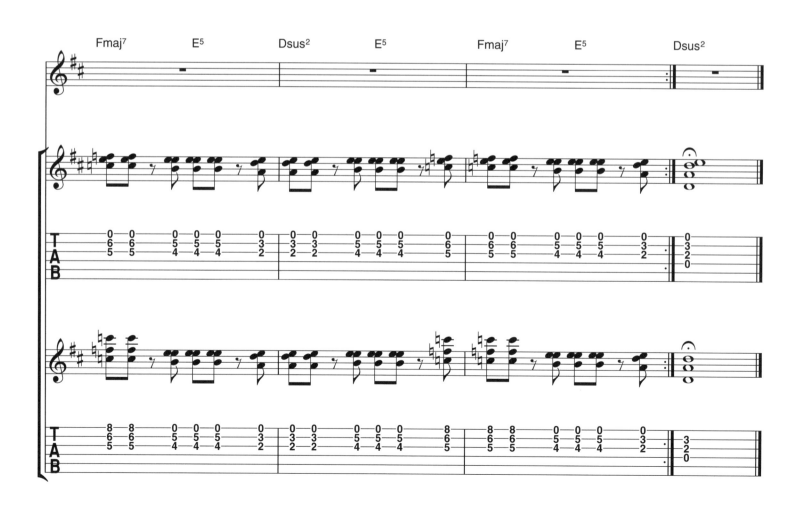

HALF THE FUN

WORDS AND MUSIC BY GARY LIGHTBODY, JONATHAN QUINN, MARK McCLELLAND AND NATHAN CONNOLLY

Chorus

GUITAR TAB GLOSSARY**

TABLATURE EXPLANATION

READING TABLATURE: Tablature illustrates the six strings of the guitar. Notes and chords are indicated by the placement of fret numbers on a given string(s).

String ⑥ **3rd** *Fret*   *String* ① **12th** *Fret*   A "C" Chord   "C" Chord Arpeggiated
String ③ **13th** *Fret*

BENDING NOTES

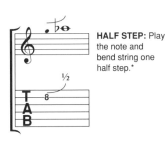

HALF STEP: Play the note and bend string one half step.*

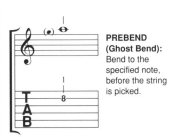

PREBEND (Ghost Bend): Bend to the specified note, before the string is picked.

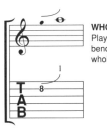

WHOLE STEP: Play the note and bend string one whole step.

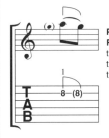

PREBEND AND RELEASE: Bend the string, play it, then release to the original note.

WHOLE STEP AND A HALF: Play the note and bend string a whole step and a half.

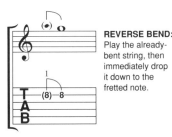

REVERSE BEND: Play the already-bent string, then immediately drop it down to the fretted note.

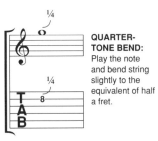

QUARTER-TONE BEND: Play the note and bend string slightly to the equivalent of half a fret.

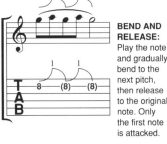

BEND AND RELEASE: Play the note and gradually bend to the next pitch, then release to the original note. Only the first note is attacked.

*A half step is the smallest interval in Western music; it is equal to one fret. A whole step equals two frets.

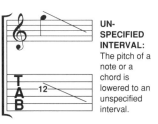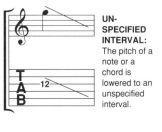

UNISON BEND: Play both notes and immediately bend the lower note to the same pitch as the higher note.

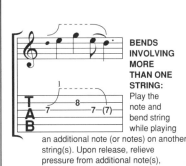

DOUBLE NOTE BEND: Play both notes and immediately bend both strings simultaneously.

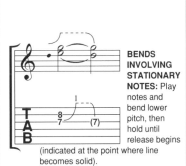

BENDS INVOLVING MORE THAN ONE STRING: Play the note and bend string while playing an additional note (or notes) on another string(s). Upon release, relieve pressure from additional note(s), causing original note to sound alone.

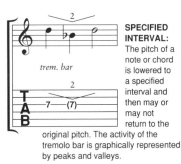

BENDS INVOLVING STATIONARY NOTES: Play notes and bend lower pitch, then hold until release begins (indicated at the point where line becomes solid).

TREMOLO BAR

SPECIFIED INTERVAL: The pitch of a note or chord is lowered to a specified interval and then may or may not return to the original pitch. The activity of the tremolo bar is graphically represented by peaks and valleys.

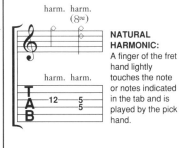

UN-SPECIFIED INTERVAL: The pitch of a note or a chord is lowered to an unspecified interval.

HARMONICS

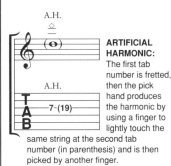

NATURAL HARMONIC: A finger of the fret hand lightly touches the note or notes indicated in the tab and is played by the pick hand.

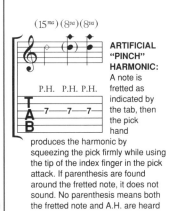

ARTIFICIAL HARMONIC: The first tab number is fretted, then the pick hand produces the harmonic by using a finger to lightly touch the same string at the second tab number (in parenthesis) and is then picked by another finger.

ARTIFICIAL "PINCH" HARMONIC: A note is fretted as indicated by the tab, then the pick hand produces the harmonic by squeezing the pick firmly while using the tip of the index finger in the pick attack. If parenthesis are found around the fretted note, it does not sound. No parenthesis means both the fretted note and A.H. are heard simultaneously.

**By Kenn Chipkin and Aaron Stang

112

RHYTHM SLASHES

STRUM INDICATIONS: Strum with indicated rhythm. The chord voicings are found on the first page of the transcription underneath the song title.

SINGLE NOTES IN SLASH NOTATION: A regular notehead indicates a single note. The circled number below the note indicates which string of the chord to strike. If the note is not in the chord, the fret number will be indicated above the note(s).

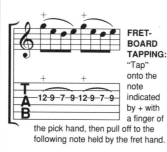

FRETBOARD TAPPING: "Tap" onto the note indicated by + with a finger of the pick hand, then pull off to the following note held by the fret hand.

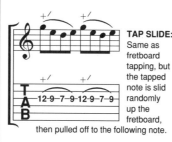

TAP SLIDE: Same as fretboard tapping, but the tapped note is slid randomly up the fretboard, then pulled off to the following note.

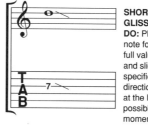

SHORT GLISSANDO: Play note for its full value and slide in specified direction at the last possible moment.

PICK SLIDE: Slide the edge of the pick in specified direction across the length of the string(s).

TRILL: Hammer on and pull off consecutively and as fast as possible between the original note and the grace note.

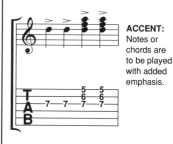

ACCENT: Notes or chords are to be played with added emphasis.

ARTICULATIONS

HAMMER ON: Play lower note, then "hammer on" to higher note with another finger. Only the first note is attacked.

LEFT HAND HAMMER: Hammer on the first note played on each string with the left hand.

PULL OFF: Play higher note, then "pull off" to lower note with another finger. Only the first note is attacked.

BEND AND TAP TECHNIQUE: Play note and bend to specified interval. While holding bend, tap onto note indicated.

LEGATO SLIDE: Play note and slide to the following note. (Only first note is attacked).

LONG GLISSANDO: Play note and slide in specified direction for the full value of the note.

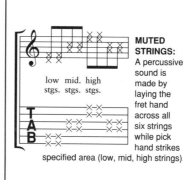

MUTED STRINGS: A percussive sound is made by laying the fret hand across all six strings while pick hand strikes specified area (low, mid, high strings).

PALM MUTE: The note or notes are muted by the palm of the pick hand by lightly touching the string(s) near the bridge.

TREMOLO PICKING: The note or notes are picked as fast as possible.

STACCATO (Detached Notes): Notes or chords are to be played roughly half their actual value and with separation.

DOWN STROKES AND UPSTROKES: Notes or chords are to be played with either a downstroke (⊓) or upstroke (ⱱ) of the pick.

VIBRATO: The pitch of a note is varied by a rapid shaking of the fret hand finger, wrist, and forearm.